CONTINGENCY, IMMANENCE, AND
THE SUBJECT OF RHETORIC

Lauer Series in Rhetoric and Composition
Series Editors: Catherine Hobbs, Patricia Sullivan, Thomas Rickert, and Jennifer Bay

The Lauer Series in Rhetoric and Composition honors the contributions Janice Lauer has made to the emergence of Rhetoric and Composition as a disciplinary study. It publishes scholarship that carries on Professor Lauer's varied work in the history of written rhetoric, disciplinarity in composition studies, contemporary pedagogical theory, and written literacy theory and research.

Books in the Series

Contingency, Immanence, and the Subject of Rhetoric (Richardson, 2013)
Rewriting Success in Rhetoric and Composition Careers (Goodburn, LeCourt, Leverenz, 2012)
Writing a Progressive Past: Women Teaching and Writing in the Progressive Era (Mastrangelo, 2012)
Greek Rhetoric Before Aristotle, 2e, Rev. and Exp. Ed. (Enos, 2012)
Rhetoric's Earthly Realm: Heidegger, Sophistry, and the Gorgian Kairos (Miller) *Winner of the Olson Award for Best Book in Rhetorical Theory 2011
Techne, from Neoclassicism to Postmodernism: Understanding Writing as a Useful, Teachable Art (Pender, 2011)
Walking and Talking Feminist Rhetorics: Landmark Essays and Controversies (Buchanan and Ryan, 2010)
Transforming English Studies: New Voices in an Emerging Genre (Ostergaard, Ludwig, and Nugent, 2009)
Ancient Non-Greek Rhetorics (Lipson and Binkley, 2009)
Roman Rhetoric: Revolution and the Greek Influence, Rev. and Exp Ed. (Enos, 2008)
Stories of Mentoring: Theory and Praxis (Eble and Gaillet, 2008)
Writers Without Borders: Writing and Teaching in Troubled Times (Bloom, 2008)
1977: A Cultural Moment in Composition (Henze, Selzer, and Sharer, 2008)
*The Promise and Perils of Writing Program Administration (*Enos and Borrowman, 2008)
Untenured Faculty as Writing Program Administrators: Institutional Practices and Politics, (Dew and Horning, 2007)
Networked Process: Dissolving Boundaries of Process and Post-Process (Foster, 2007)
Composing a Community: A History of Writing Across the Curriculum (McLeod and Soven, 2006)
Historical Studies of Writing Program Administration: Individuals, Communities, and the Formation of a Discipline (L'Eplattenier and Mastrangelo, 2004). Winner of the WPA Best Book Award for 2004–2005.
Rhetorics, Poetics, and Cultures: Refiguring College English Studies Exp. Ed. (Berlin, 2003)

CONTINGENCY, IMMANENCE, AND THE SUBJECT OF RHETORIC

Timothy Richardson

Parlor Press
Anderson, South Carolina
www.parlorpress.com

Parlor Press LLC, Anderson, South Carolina, USA

© 2013 by Parlor Press
All rights reserved.
Printed in the United States of America

SAN: 254-8879

Library of Congress Cataloging-in-Publication Data

Richardson, Timothy, 1969-
  Immanence, and the Subject of Rhetoric / Timothy Richardson.
    pages cm. -- (The Lauer Series in Rhetoric and Composition)
  Includes bibliographical references and index.
  ISBN 978-1-60235-363-3 (pbk. : acid-free paper) -- ISBN 978-1-60235-364-0 (hardcover : acid-free paper) -- ISBN 978-1-60235-365-7 (adobe ebook) -- ISBN 978-1-60235-366-4 (epub)
 1. Rhetoric. 2. Immanence of God in literature. 3. Rhetoric and psychology. 4. Causation in literature. 5. Rhetoric--Religious aspects. I. Title.
  P301.R54 2013
  808--dc23
                              2013031676

1 2 3 4 5

Cover photo, "Heavenly Light" by Greg Glau. See gglau.zenfolio.com for more of Greg's photography. Greg Glau is the Official Photographer of Parlor Press.
Cover design by David Blakesley. Copyediting by Laura Batson, Brian Bowers, Patrick Clarke, Benjamin Cousins, Andrew Harris, Cody Lang, Karl Lykken, Courtney Mohan, Cleveland Noel, Patrick O'Friel, Melanie Payne, Connor Pencek, Parag Raychoudhury, Michael Wooten, and Devin Wrigley
Printed on acid-free paper.

Parlor Press, LLC is an independent publisher of scholarly and trade titles in print and multimedia formats. This book is available in paper, cloth and Adobe eBook formats from Parlor Press on the World Wide Web at http://www.parlorpress.com or through online and brick-and-mortar bookstores. For submission information or to find out about Parlor Press publications, write to Parlor Press, 3015 Brackenberry Drive, Anderson, South Carolina, 29621, or email editor@parlorpress.com.

For Laura and Benjamin and Harper, who are my causes

Contents

Forward   ix

Acknowledgments   xiii

Introduction   3

1 An Image to Honor and Worship   17

2 Rhetoric as Mitzvah   45

3 But the Greatest of These Is Love   74

4 Nothing But the Effects of Those Instances of Saying   101

5 What Stops Not Being Written   126

Notes   153

Works Cited   163

Index   169

About the Author   173

Forward

David Metzger

The phrase "It is not in heaven" (*lo bashayim hi*) appears once in the Hebrew Bible (*Deuteronomy/Devarim* 30:12). The *Babylonian Talmud* makes reference to it on six occasions or so (Eruvin 55a., Bava Metzia 59b). And we find six references to it in *Midrash Rabbah*, most of which are in *Devarim Rabbah*, a compilation of rabbinic commentaries on the book of *Deuteronomy*. Contemporary scholars and community leaders (from Chaim Perelman to Rabbi Walter Homolka) have made good use of the phrase as an anchor or authorization for their discussions of the unique expansiveness of rabbinic discourse where minority opinions and multiple voices are valued and preserved. Presumably, if "it" is not in heaven, then it is for us to decide and act–at least inasmuch as the majority of us can be rendered as a "universal audience" or "social conscience."

The "it" is expressed variously within this corpus: sometimes it is "this mitzvah"; sometimes it is "the Torah"; in other instances, it is simply "knowing what to do or knowing what is right." For Richardson, the "it" is rhetoric. Rhetoric is not in heaven, and—in this manner—he reorients rhetoric's ontological narrative (at least the one that begins with Plato and Aristotle) into an examination not of how rhetoric has been marginalized but how its apparently beleaguered state has functioned as a necessary gap/relationship between word and thing, fiction and reality, transcendence and immanence, religion and history, desire and jouissance, Judaism and Christianity. Not only is this gap necessary, it is so necessary that it takes on the characteristics of a relationship and, as such, reinvigorates the question, "What is the rhetorical subject?" And it prompts us to ask "What is the Other for rhetoric?"

With this second question, *Contingency, Immanence, and the Subject of Rhetoric* introduces readers to a bold concept, what I would call the "God of the Rhetoric." Using the work of Jacques Lacan and Kenneth Burke, Richardson develops Aristotle's basic description of the four causes (efficient, material, formal, final) into an argument regarding the Subject/Other/God of Christian and Jewish texts. He introduces, as well, a method for reading the necessary gap/relationship of these texts. Richardson's treatment of the four causes provides a language with which to identify our attraction and engagement with texts lest and so that we might recognize the relationship/gap between our engagement with texts and our engagement with ourselves and others.

Each chapter brings its own original and welcome contribution. Chapter 1 resituates the familiar notion of negative theology in the work of Kenneth Burke, showing how rhetoric (understood as a way of working the negative in language) obviates the divide between the God of Philosophy and the God of Religion in both Augustinian and rabbinic discourse. Chapter 2's focus on history and memory as ways to construct the Other is wonderfully accessible, and the Rabbinic texts selected as examples are the bread and butter of any Introduction to Rabbinics course. Chapter 3 juxtaposes Girard, Kristeva, Burke, and Kierkegaard's reading of the binding of Isaac (the aquedah)—not only adding to our knowledge of each but explaining their attraction and engagement with narratives of sacrifice as attempts to create a good (enough) Other. Chapter 4 puts all of chapter 3's important theoretical work to good purpose by offering a powerful and insightful reading of "The Chronicle of Solomon bar Simson," a Jewish account of the Crusades. And Chapter 5 gives us our homework. How does the rhetorical engage us?: "If the rhetoric is going to (re)discover the contingent nature of its subject, it can only do so by turning back from the philosophical, by becoming its mirror image, by taking the place of the cause for its subject in order to imply in the subject what the subject cannot say but nonetheless performs daily."

What does this have to do with our engagement with ourselves and others? And who, by the way, is this us you keep talking about? Given that sacrifice and love often find their home in the gaps/relationships identified in the texts Richardson discusses, it is possible to see that these gaps/relationships might also be blind spots for those who call for or valorize the bliss of suffering in their identification of heroes and heroines. To be sure, *Contingency, Immanence, and the Subject of*

Rhetoric does not explicitly aim to recover and value the silenced voices of the past to create a vision of a better future. But its attentiveness to rabbinic notions of textuality does bring Jewish texts into the ongoing conversation about rhetoric. And it does so without invoking the ocular equivalent of "entering into a conversation," which bears all the evil that good conversation will not abide: the promise of safety through surveillance. For those of us who are concerned that, in developing a Jewish rhetoric over and against a Hellenic one, we must be careful not to see or only be seen by what emerges from that gap/relationship, the discovery of the rhetorical subject's contingent nature is a comforting and promising thought.

Acknowledgments

From the very start, I need to give special thanks to David Metzger, who has been the model I look to for work and everything else. Also, huge thanks to Ellie Ragland, Allen Frantzen, Christopher Kendrick, James Biester, and Steven Jones for their tutelage, advice, and encouragement. Thanks to Levi Bryant, Kenneth Reinhard, Victor Vitanza, Nathan Gale, David Purkiss, Aprell Feagin, and my colleagues at the University of Texas at Arlington for coffee and support. To my parents and—since a good cast is worth repeating—to Laura and Harper and Ben, thank you for your love and help.

I would also like to thank *Pre/Text* for allowing me to expand "Love is a Battlefield: Sacrifice, the Abject, and Better Parenting Through Lying" for the third chapter [*Pre/Text* 19.2 (2009): 97-120]. And thanks to *JAC* for permission to weave "Writing (and Doing) Trauma Study" into the final two chapters [*JAC* 24 (2004): 491-507].

Of course, it is impossible to recognize by name everyone who deserves my gratitude. I am indebted to every book I've read, each ear I've bent, all those friends who have been patient, and all those to whom I owe dinner or beer.

Contingency, Immanence, and the Subject of Rhetoric

Introduction

> *The other world surrounds us always and it is not at all at the end of some pilgrimage. In our earthly house, windows are replaced by mirrors; the door, until a given time, is closed; but air comes in through the cracks.*
>
> —Vladimir Nabokov, *The Gift*

Since I promise an academic inquiry concerned with rhetoric, rabbis, and psychoanalysis, it may seem odd to begin with an epigraph from this dense novelist of the last century. But the following is also a discussion about writing and reading. Nabokov both wrote and read. I had considered other quotes, but what struck me about the lines above is that, in his greatest Russian novel (a narrative, a story), Nabokov makes what appears to be an overtly religious appeal. He assumes—or has his character assume—that there is another world. This in part keeps with one of his overall questions: How does time (really, memory and history) reconcile itself with space and the obvious *here-ness of a situation?*[1] And, so, what can be written that isn't simply *what is, right now*? Put another way, can we read Nabokov's and any number of other texts as probes toward some kind of transcendence, toward what is true because it is guaranteed by something else? For Nabokov, this Something Else is a purely speculative other world. For Plato, it is the realm of Forms. For Augustine, God in heaven. For us, the guarantee might be found in language or culture or something else just as pervasive-seeming. The point is that there is a tendency to assume an extrinsic and essentially separate ground not only for What Is, but for What Is Possible.

Or we might think of Nabokov's lines as a statement on the nature of fiction. A pilgrimage is, in a manner of speaking, a narrative. If we assume for the moment the notion of time as the measurement of the movement of a body through space, this makes sense. The ground for the trip would be the destination, at least in its potentiality, as a kind of final cause. Such is what Chaucer wrote for us. The genius of Chaucer is not the trip, though, but the stories the traveling characters tell and what these stories tell us about them. Even in Chaucer's time, there were conventions for the telling of stories. Thus, narrative itself can be a ground, too, especially for those stories involved with confession.[2] This is a simple but important point. To tell any story also means to talk about yourself.

When I was very young, my family would pray before meals. We would close our eyes and bow our heads. Once (and only once) after the prayer I told my parents that my sister hadn't closed her eyes, that she hadn't actually *prayed*. You can see the problem with that.

As far as writing goes, there is another peculiarity. I can actually remember my younger self's realization that the authors of some of the books I was reading were dead. Really, it hadn't occurred to me that they would be. The books were still there and my experiences of them were so immediate, even my used book-club *Bend Sinister* (Nabokov was the first author I loved) seemed so contemporary, so immediate, that the writers just had to be. They were like me, since they probably wrote the kinds of things they wanted to read, and I wanted to read them, too. And if they were like me, they must be alive. I am alive. Of course, I likely didn't reason it out that way, but was simply surprised. Then, perhaps I shrugged. There is something about writing that is alive regardless of the author's fitness. The author, as Cervantes almost said, is the son of his work. Of course, the fact of an author's death might add some sense of entitlement to that author's work, so death might itself be considered an extrinsic ground for canonization, say, or for serious study.

(Contrast this with a recent student's happy realization that "literature" is still being written by relatively young and healthy people. There are new stories.)

In some ways, even very old writing is present. Both T. S. Eliot and Harold Bloom make this point.[3] We worship our ancestors because the dead are always with us. They surround us, since for them the doors have opened. And we find ourselves on our knees, heads down, trying to breathe what comes clear of the cracks beneath the closed ones: a common position for both prayer and scholarship.

I. The Problem

Concerning the extrinsic ground, Kenneth Burke writes: "For 'pure persuasion' is an absolute, logically prior to any persuasive act. It is the essence of language. And just as the over-all Title of Titles is a 'god-term,' so persuasion in all purity would transform courtship into prayer, not prayer for an end, but prayer for its own sake (*Rhetoric of Motives 252*). Here we find some moves similar to Nabokov's. Again, there is a direct appeal to something divine, something on which everything—or at least everything that can be said—is based. True, Burke seems to posit a hierarchical relation, whereas Nabokov prefers a simple inside/outside binary. But both avoid pinning truth (they are both discussing truth) to contingency.

Persuasion, writes Burke, is logically—not temporally—prior to an act. And an act might be understood as taking place *in time under certain conditions*. On one hand, these conditions are a certain context that is contingent, since it need not necessarily happen this way. On the other hand, an act is inscribed as/in history, since afterward (say, when we close the book) it seems it could only have happened this way, given that the act defines a particular time as an object, as a *then* against a *now*. But the essence of rhetorical language is outside the scope of context/contingency inasmuch as it must exist prior to the act that is both described by and defines its moment in/as history.

However, Burke's third sentence throws us back into the temporal, as he introduces persuasion's transformational powers. The product of persuasion is prayer, but not "prayer for an end." The pilgrimage is not important. Or, rather, pilgrimage is all that is important, but arriving somewhere is not. Consider the labyrinths in some old English churches which the elderly or infirmed would walk in lieu of taking the trek to Jerusalem. Can we say that they arrived anywhere? We certainly cannot say that they arrived nowhere. And since they didn't arrive nowhere, they must have arrived somewhere. That is simply logical.

More generally, how can we actually say anything at all? And how can we say something true? And what about writing it all down?[4] That is, what is at the top—or the bottom—of this pyramid? What guarantees that we can even ask these questions? The impetus for the following inquiry came from the simple recognition that, in the tradition of what I will call Greco-Christian Rhetoric, few seem to be able to avoid pointing to an Ultimate as a guarantee, or to avoid at least talking about something like the Prime Mover, Christ, Culture and History, or the Other, all gods being equal. So one question here is, "Why can't rhetoricians do without God?"

Of course, there are all sorts of other concerns connected to this question. If we were doing a brainstorming activity—say, clustering—we could write the word "God" in the middle of a piece of paper, circle it, then draw lines to circles containing things like "Aristotelian Prime Mover," "Platonic Forms," "Christ," "The Other," etc. And from these terms we might go to "logical and temporal priority," "Holy Scripture," "The Church," "History," "Love," "Sacrifice," even "Teaching." And so on. Of course, we know that one challenge clustering does not eliminate is how to take all this emanation and lay it out logically so that meaning unfolds gradually. In practice, I may write out each word or phrase one at a time, as I go, but when I arrive at my cluster and take it as a whole, my job is then to ask, as Talking Heads ask, "How did I get here?" I then begin to take the structure apart and arrange it logically, as an argument for the diagram, producing an "as I go" without any real consideration of reproducing the "as I went." And we know that this *as we go* is really not simply logical, since writing and reading are temporal activities, too, as one word leads to another. Just like a story.

II. THE PLOT

What follows is a pilgrimage of sorts. That is, there is both a logical and temporal journey made, as long as we realize that the ultimate goal, an answer to the question "Do rhetoricians need God?" might be less important finally than recognizing what happens when we assume an ultimate and what ultimates we tend to assume, what rare air comes through the cracks. The question might really be "How do rhetoricians use God?" or "What is the rhetorical God?" In one sense, this book traces a path from the ancient and late antique Western world to contemporary concerns about representation. In another sense, the book tries to find its way from metaphysics to praxis, which is to say, from courtship to prayer to…something else.

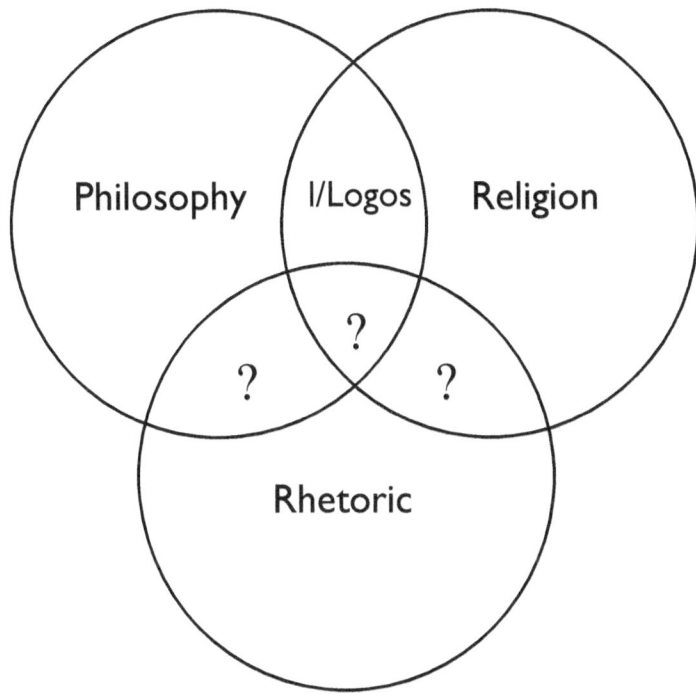

Figure 1. Philosophy / Religion / Rhetoric. Illustration by the author.

I imagine a kind of borromean knot with fields marked as Philosophy, Religion, and Rhetoric. My concern is to demonstrate in what sense Rhetoric is born from and offers a critique of the Philosophy/Religion overlap via a shift from the extrinsic (positive) cause (*the necessity* of an extrinsic cause is how I define the religious generally) to the extimate (traumatic, abject, historical) cause. That is, how might it be possible to reverse what Lacan says about love as the turn from contingency (*what stops not being written*) to necessity (*what doesn't stop being written*), as love is a sign that one is changing discourses? Rhetoric is insinuated/implied between the one (philosophy) and the one (religion) either as the Other or as the object cause of desire.

There are several reasons for turning to Rabbinic Judaism as a critique of the Greco-Christian. First, wherever there are Christians, there are Jews. This is probably obvious, but it does seem worthwhile to point out that one needn't go very far afield geographically to find rhetorics against which to measure the standard Western *recit*. And the form of Judaism that eventually became orthodox became ascendant at approximately the same time as orthodox Christianity and in dialogue with it (Boyarin 374). In asserting this, I am primarily following Daniel Boyarin in *Border Lines: The Partition of Judaeo-Christianity* and elsewhere. More generally, interest into how the received Classical (read Greek and Roman, if not Christian) tradition may have found its way into or against rabbinic thought and practice is of recent interest to several scholars. Richard Hidary claims:

> I propose that elements of rhetorical thinking and its methodologies were widespread throughout the Greco-Roman world and formed an integral part of its culture. The rabbis may have absorbed these ideas in conversations with neighbors or through listening to an orator in a public square. Whatever the case, the classical canons formed the basis of thought and composition throughout the Roman Empire, and the rabbis could not have been completely isolated from them. (37)

Hidary's position seems reasonable to me. It is less direct than Boyarin's, and while I prefer the latter's hard dating to more general questions of influence, the trend to read rabbinic and Classical source with and against each other is a growing and compelling one.[5]

So, since it should become apparent in later chapters that Lacanian psychoanalysis (the reigning theoretical apparatus of this book) and Rabbinic Judaism (as a historical precedent) share a great deal in common in terms of their responses to the Greek and Christian tradition, the rabbis offer a good (and subaltern) lineage for the kinds of thought I am advocating.

Additionally, the project of this book is to offer an understanding of rhetoric that depends on a pun: *a*-theism. This rhetoric shouldn't be considered secular in the simple sense that it ignores the religious (as an appeal to an extrinsic cause), but rather it seeks to find a place for the religious within its practice. That is, rhetoric should allow for the religious while at the same time not assuming it as a cause.

Or, consider the following long passage from Daniel Boyarin:

> In the end, it is not the case that Christianity and Judaism are two separate or different religions, but that they are two different kinds of things altogether. From the point of view of the

> Church's category formation, Judaism and Christianity...are examples of the category religions, one a bad example and the other a very good one, indeed the only prototype. But from the point of view of the Rabbis' categorization, Christianity is a religion and Judaism is not. Judaism remains a religion for the Church because, I will suggest, it is a necessary moment in the construction of Christian orthodoxy and thus Christian religion, whereas occasional and partial Jewish appropriations of the name and status of religion are strategic, mimetic, and contingent. Like the layerings of the unconscious or the interpenetrating stratifications of Roman material culture that so inspired Freud, however, the vaunted ambivalence of Judaism is, I suggest, a product of that history, of that partial acceptance and then almost total refusal of the option of orthodoxy and heresy as the Jews' mode of self-definition—the refusal, that is, finally to become a religion. (13)

Rabbinic Judaism's flirtation with the appellation religion ends with an ambivalence that mirrors rhetoric's choice of contingency over philosophic necessity. In fact, if we reread the preceding citation, replacing *Christianity* with *philosophy* and *Judaism* with *rhetoric*, I think we also get a pretty clear picture of the ancient tensions between philosophy and rhetoric and the anxiety the latter has provoked in the former. Rhetoric has always been a problem for philosophy precisely because, to a very large extent, philosophy needed rhetoric for its self-definition. And rhetoric has always had a "strategic, mimetic, and contingent" relationship with the philosophy.

The first chapter begins with a reading of the nature of rhetoric with Plato and a meditation on Aristotle's understanding of the rhetorical art, followed by a discussion of how Augustine is able to co-opt the Aristotelian Mover and transform philosophy into Christianity. This chapter—through Kenneth Burke and David Metzger, among others—addresses problems of causality and the definition of love as an elaboration of logos, indicates how these standard rhetorical texts situate the subject in terms of an extrinsic cause qua Mover or Deity, and demonstrates how the presumption of a formal, necessary cause determines a particular notion of history. Against this particular understanding of causation we are then able to place the rabbinic counterargument.

In the second chapter, I position the nature of the text in late antique Rabbinic Judaism (specifically the redactions of the Babylonian Talmud and Midrash as we have them now) in contrast to the Greco-Christian problem of causality and history. I argue (along with Daniel Boyarin's recent work) that the rabbis, against the logos of Greco-Christianity, place the apparatus of a text that is contingent and wholly cultural. The result is an insistence of contemporaneity and immanence against the necessary and formal. Certainly, there are many differences between Christianity and Judaism, and my proposition is that one of the most important differences—indeed, the one on which the others depend—is what is assumed as the foundation for being: logos or text.

It should be stressed here that I am not simply arguing for an exchange of the Greco-Christian tradition for a rabbinic one, but am claiming that the former has always been privileged over the latter. If we can (at least sometimes) assume a contingent, even immanent position regarding causality, then we might say, along with Lacan, that "[r]eality is approached with the apparatuses of jouissance . . . [and] there's no apparatus other than language" (*Encore*, Lacan 150). With Lacan, as with Nabokov, we find pilgrimage in the notion of approaching reality, but with our foregrounding the trip over any destination. Reality is approached, but likely asymptotically. With Lacan, though, the divine is sidestepped. Language is an apparatus, a means by which one gets at reality. And by reality I suppose he does not mean the Lacanian Real, but the (symbolic) structures that surround us, those things—or that thing—we might call humanity, culture or, in another system, God. Along with Burke, though, Lacan privileges language as an object of a study. The difference between them is, it seems, a semantic one. Burke writes *prayer*. Lacan is always speaking of *jouissance*.

If reality is approached through the apparatuses of jouissance, if there is no apparatus other than language, and if the essence of language is outside the temporal, contingent nature of the act, then there is both a necessary extrinsic ground for the possibility of, say, relating an event or telling a story, and there is something inherent in the act of doing these things that participates in the contingent nature of them while always/already covering over the very fact of their contingency. This ground for some is something like God, and, for others, the assumption of language itself.

So, Lacan links language with jouissance, Burke associates it with prayer, and both jouissance and prayer are considered in the third chapter, first by way of a discussion of René Girard's and Julia Kristeva's understanding of the relations of logos with love, prayer, and sacrifice and finally in Burke's reading of Kierkegaard's rereading of the Binding of Isaac. The chapter is a kind of case study for the Greco-Christian position that takes love as an ultimate term and looks closely at it and the stories we (must) tell to make love work.

Whereas the first three chapters deal primarily with the written in terms of heuristics, the fourth begins to apply the previous discussions to questions of writing. Where the first and second chapters address a history of thought and hermeneutics, this chapter calls into question the nature of history itself, arguing that histories/stories/narratives are not simply modes of excavating causes and meanings but function *necessarily and at the same time* as ways of screening present concerns with the veil of time. That is, the positive ultimate term (the extrinsic first cause, perhaps sacrifice) is here replaced by the experience of substantive lack, allowing for a secularization. Omnipresent God and the power of Love become, in this new scheme, a necessary or formal lack constituted by the symbolic order itself.

So, lack. Certainly, there has been a great deal of work critiquing the idea of lack as constitutive or even useful in or for philosophy, rhetoric, etc.[6] The dispute, I think, hinges on a misunderstanding in which some readers imagine Lacan arguing for an inherent lack in the symbolic order as such. Rather, Lacan's position seems to be concerned with how the symbolic order generates the conditions for a perceived lack—for the neurotic, for instance, who constantly asks "Who am I (for the Other)?" How is it that, in a universe which by definition lacks nothing, a subjectivity emerges in which lack is experienced? I will address some of these issues later in the fifth chapter, but for now it might be useful to suggest that, for instance, the Lacanian gospel *il n'y a pas de rapport sexuel* means that there is no complementary relationship. Both sides miss each other as the masculine relies on transcendence (an extrinsic cause) and the feminine on immanence (see the second chapter and later), a situation that is constituted or manufactured by the symbolic and not something inherent to it. That is, I may feel like I cannot find a suitable partner, that one is lacking from my life, but this perceived lack is really a product of all sorts of positive expectations bolstered by film and other romans and is a function of fantasy, which satisfies by way of a constant (and productive) dissatisfaction. This is one way of imagining the function of the object cause of desire, as that which is immanently productive but necessarily unsatisfying. The final argument of this book has to do with the morphing of the extrinsic cause (as an exception, which is the basis of both philosophy and Christianity) to an extimate cause (*as objet a,* a foreign kernel inside the subject, which leads to a wholly *a*-theistic accounting of rhetoric). The experience of lack as a positive and foreign presence is the mechanism by which such change occurs.

Put another way, contrary to some readings, Giles Deleuze is not an enemy of lack. In a discussion of virtual objects (which are much like Kleinian partial objects and very much like Lacan's *objet a*) in *Difference and Repetition*, Deleuze maintains:

> Although it is deducted from the present real object, the virtual object differs from it in kind: not only does it lack something in relation to the real object from which it is subtracted, it lacks something in itself, since it is always half of itself, the other half being different as well as absent. This absence, as we shall see, is the opposite of a negative. Eternal half of itself, it is where it is only on condition that it is not where it should be. It is where we find it only on the condition that we search for it where it is not. It is at once not possessed by those who have it and had by those who do not possess it. It is always a "was." In this sense, Lacan's pages assimilating the virtual object to Edgar Allen Poe's purloined letter seem to us exemplary. (102)

The letter is where it is, which also means that the letter's absence from its *proper* place is what motivates, well, everyone. Lack as an absence indicates that the symbolic order makes a place for something that is misplaced. For instance, we might say that a given library book simply is wherever it is, and that it is only in reference to a catalog that a book can be missing or out of place; the catalog generates a place on the shelf for a book to hold whether or not the book occupies it, and the lack of the book in the library is derived therefrom.[7]

To return to the religious, Lacan makes much the same point in his Seminar VII:

> The potter makes a pot starting with a clay that is more or less fine or refined; and it is at this point that our religious preach-

> ers stop us, so as to make us hear the moaning of the vase in the potter's hand. The preacher makes it talk in the most moving of ways, even to the point of moaning, and makes it ask its creator why he treats it so roughly or, on the contrary, so gently. But what is masked in this example of creationist mythology...is that the vase is made from matter. Nothing is made from nothing. (*Ethics* 121)

There is no prior and inherent lack, but rather the symbolic order as such produces gaps as signifiers that are separated from each other (land and water, light and dark in the first Genesis creation story, for instance) in any attempt to carve the real into something manageable.[8] There is something that resists symbolization, something that is nonetheless always being talked about, such that "the fashioning of a signifier and the introduction of a gap or a hole in the real is identical." (121).

Years ago, as a graduate student, I took a course on portfolio construction and grading. The final assignment was to collect all of the written graduate work I had completed up to that point (my history) and reread the essays in order to discover what questions and ideas I continually returned to, regardless of the assignment. That is, the job was to look for what I was always *writing about* without worrying about what I was actually *writing*. Much in the same way a potter throws a pot from the clay at hand and molds the material around an absence she creates, this portfolio assignment might finally be a way of discovering my dissertation topic. In fact, the real work was deconstructing those texts in order to discover what I really wanted to talk about, but was always trying not to talk about. This last is the jouissance of writing. I imagine that trying not to say something is what keeps much of our work moving along.

Anyway, along with a consideration of Lacan's insights on history, then, are discussions of the formative nature of trauma and (following Cathy Caruth's reading) of Sigmund Freud's *Moses and Monotheism* as a fresh kind of historical document. The chapter ends with another case study, the *Hebrew Chronicle of the First Crusade*, with an eye toward discovering a/the jouissance of writing as history in terms of what such jouissance must cover in order to say something about an event, to indicate something that we can call trauma.

The fifth chapter translates the discussion of lack and trauma, in relation to history, into the structure of discourse. I then argue that a rabbinically-psychoanalytically inspired theory of rhetoric is best able to account for what is not spoken but is nevertheless always being spoken about. I return to discussions of love and cause—now with a psychoanalytic inflection—to argue that the rhetorical project is the in(ter)jection of cause into the subject of analysis. Both rhetorical display and rhetorical analysis generate their own causes that retroactively situate the subject (the audience and author, the text) such that the subject is moved from the necessary, formal position of looking outward toward a static cause into a field of immanence and contingency, what I am calling an extimate cause. It is from within this field that change can take place.

III. The Present

So, Nabokov claims that another world surrounds us. I am happy with the epigraph; the widows as mirrors are evocative of early Jacques Lacan, and I like Nabokov's reworking of Plato's cave. It's not a question of seeing, but of smelling the evidence. As we all know, smell is closely associated with memory. And there is some kind of relationship between memory and history. So, we can smell the other world? Under this definition, the writer might be a kind of perfumer, a *nose*, *s*omeone who selects fragrances from the world and combines them to create something pleasing.

But if the other world surrounds us always, do we need to assume a Great Perfumer, or can it be that the world simply has a smell, even several smells, depending on how the wind blows? The Greco-Christian position is that God makes the odors for us. The floral ground means a flower somewhere. The early rabbinic assumption is, perhaps, that we are really interpreting the vagaries of wind.

There were other bits from Nabokov I had considered for an epigraph. In the short story "Ultima Thule," Nabokov has his hero argue:

> By the very act of your mentioning a given concept you placed your own self in the position of an enigma, as if the seeker himself were to hide. And by persisting in your question, you not only hide, but also believe that by sharing with the sought-for object the quality of "hiddenness" you bring it closer to you. How can I answer you whether God exists when

the matter under discussion is perhaps sweet peas or a soccer linesman's flag? (*Russian Beauty* 175)

The difficulty, it seems, is that the philosopher tries to hide himself from the search, as if the seeker—by virtue of his disinterest, his removal—can summon the object closer to him via a deification of the concept. The seeker, the subject, is an absent cause. But, "[t]he absurdity at which searching thought arrives is only a natural, generic sign of its belonging to man, and striving to obtain an answer is the same as demanding of chicken broth that it began [sic] to cluck" (*Gift* 354).

On the other hand, and against this absurdity, Nabokov suggests that the creative writer works from impossible standards which consist of

> the supremacy of the detail over the general, of the part that is more alive than the whole, of the little thing which a man observes and greets with a friendly nod of the spirit while the crowd around him is being driven by some common impulse to some common goal.... This capacity to wonder at trifles—no matter the imminent peril—these footnotes in the volume of life are the highest forms of consciousness. (373-74)

It is this fascination with the specific that I find valuable in both rabbinic and psychoanalytic work, and while the rabbis would no doubt disagree with the appellation "trifle," they would certainly appreciate the footnotes. It is literally what they write.

Of course, none of these quotes was quite *contained* enough for an epigraph. But a final consideration is from my favorite of Nabokov's novels, *Bend Sinister*, and has the benefit of evoking time, images and habits of the mind: "Certain mind pictures have become so adulterated by the concept of 'time' that we have come to believe in the actual existence of a *permanently moving* bright fissure (the point of perception) between our retrospective eternity which we cannot recall and the prospective one which we cannot know" (155). His point of contention is, I take it, with the notion that the fissure is permanently moving, which seems to be impossible. But this fissure—what I will later call the gap or bar that creates and defines both rabbinic textuality and the Lacanian subject —*is* the subject of enunciation, the subject of and for rhetoric, bound as it is to the present. The fissure, then, replaces the crack mentioned in the opening epigraph and becomes my central metaphor, following the logic of the cut or bar in the Lacanian flavor of psychoanalysis. What I am interested in throughout this book are those fissures that exist (as we encounter them) between what is written and the reading/writing of it. The cause of reading, of writing, of history, of being "is not in heaven," which is precisely what allows for its insistent presence now.

1 An Image to Honor and Worship

> *Since the rhetorician offers to speak and to write about everything, and the philosopher tries to think about everything, they have always been rivals in their claim to provide a universal training of the mind. This rivalry appeared in Plato's polemic against the Sophists; it continued throughout the later centuries of Greek antiquity . . . it was largely forgotten among the Romans and their successors in the early Middle Ages . . . it reappeared in various ways in the high Middle Ages with the rise of philosophical studies, and again in the Renaissance when humanistic learning began to compete with the scholastic tradition of Aristotelian philosophy.*
>
> —P. O. Kristeller

When Kristeller suggests that "the rhetorician offers to speak and write about everything, and the philosopher tries to think about everything," our attention should be drawn not to the apparent object of both inquiries—the "everything"—but to the modes, the methods, the processes, and the verbs. That is, philosophers (try to) think. Rhetoricians (offer to) speak and write.

Often the above position is taken to indicate that philosophy is situated prior to rhetoric. One must have knowledge in order to disseminate/demonstrate (about everything) and rhetoric proper is mostly the ability to organize knowledge and make it presentable. Rhetoric dresses knowledge up for an audience, makes truth attractive for polite circles.

It may be that any hermeneutic question is primarily a philosophical question. Since my investigations here seek in part to trouble suppositions of grounds of for reading and writing, it should be useful to

17

see where we have come from, what still remains, and what options there might be in Western hermeneutics.

Certainly, much could be made of mapping a great tradition of Western thought moving from the ancient Greeks to the present, with significant signposts marking transitions to Christianity while maintaining a predominantly Greco-Roman disposition. Aquinas is often credited with refurbishing Aristotle for Christians, for keeping him relevant. Augustine could not give up his Roman rhetoric even despite his soul-searching. Indeed, Kenneth Burke suggests that one might plot a curve from Aristotle (through Cicero, Quintilian and Longinus) to Augustine's restoration of "the dignity of rhetoric" (*Rhetoric of Motives* 74, 76). But this restoration causes an oddity; the necessary shift in the ground for rhetoric is precisely what makes the restoration Christian.

A question arises as to the possibility of an object for rhetoric other than the dissemination of philosophy or the propagation of religion qua Christianity. That is, does or can rhetoric—for the rhetorician especially—address a cause that is not a borrowed cause? Presuming the answer is yes, where might we find the cause of rhetoric in relation to these other two great and historic enterprises? In what sense might rhetoricians participate in (instead of merely describe) the tensions intrinsic to the philosophical and the religious incarnations of their objects—logos or Christ, the word or the Word—and what might rhetoric offer in their place? Put another way, what is there to speaking and writing as performance that is not, essentially, thinking? If rhetoric is not thought, what is it and what is it always talking about?

This book is an exploration of another accounting of the place and object of rhetorical inquiry in terms of what will finally be described as an extimate cause. Rhetoric as a practice may be that which addresses the contingent, foreign element internal to the subject (of discussion, of enunciation, etc.) in contrast to those philosophical and religious modes that are founded upon a necessary and extrinsic cause that delimits the set of possible understandings (of the subject and of the world) and forces us toward a *grand récit*. There is, of course, a long way to go. First, then, a version of the Classical traced from Plato to Augustine.

I. GROUNDS

If we begin (as is the custom) with Plato, the object of the philosopher is knowledge. Dialectic, as the tool of philosophy, is the mode of discovering available means through which one might get at truth.

In the *Gorgias*, Socrates's contention is that rhetoric as it is practiced has no necessary ground in knowledge, at least as its goal is to sway listeners toward some preselected conclusion. Rhetoric has its answers before any talking begins. Socrates asks Gorgias with what knowledge rhetoric is concerned. Gorgias responds that it is concerned with knowledge of words. But, with Socrates' guidance, we discover along with Gorgias that rhetoric is not concerned with all qualities or functions of words (or with their natures, say, which are conventional), but with their use to persuade. Rhetoric is the art of persuasion, and Gorgias is forced to allow that rhetoric's aim is not knowledge but belief (454c-d). Eventually Gorgias admits that the preferred audience for rhetoric, the swaying of which is the supposed goal, is in fact the ignorant. The point to be made here is that, for Plato's Socrates, the end of rhetoric is not a move toward some knowledge or even understanding, but simply the swaying of popular opinion. Hence rhetoric has no techne, is not an art, since, as George A. Kennedy puts it, "true arts are always based on knowledge and aim at the good" (Kennedy 49). To Socrates, the *knack* of the rhetoric Gorgias and company propose aims at flattery and at pleasure, certainly not any kind of knowledge.

Through discussions with the next three participants, Socrates hones his arguments, becomes more particular and, in the end, makes his point more forcefully than the others. Of course he wins the arguments; the text is not an account, but a demonstration of what is being argued *qua* the possibility of rhetoric:
1. Rhetoric as professed by the four is a tool to sway the ignorant, not a method of addressing knowledge (459b-c).
2. Thus, rhetoric is not an art, but flattery, since true arts are based on knowledge and aim at the good and rhetoric *as it is practiced* is based on experience and aims at pleasure (see the celebrated cooking analogy) (462b-466a). [9]
3. A true philosophical rhetoric does not exist, but if it did, if rhetoric could become techne, then such an orator would look to truth when

> [H]e applies to people's souls whatever speeches he makes as well as all of his actions, and any gift he makes or any confiscation he carries out. He will always give his attention to how justice may come to exist in the souls of his fellow citizens and injustice be gotten rid of, how self-control may come to exist there and lack of discipline be gotten rid of, and how the rest of excellence may come into being there and badness may depart. (504d-e)

Even with this last possibility, rhetoric remains a tool to sway an audience. Philosophy is the ground for rhetoric. A good rhetor is someone who knows the truth prior to speaking. Citizens need to be led and the leader, Plato maintains, should be wise and should have knowledge already. To modify Shakespeare somewhat: The truth will out as long as someone, ghost or philosopher, already knows it.[10]

The Socrates of Plato's *Phaedrus* is kinder to the rhetorician. He allows that rhetoric may be an art as it leads the soul by means of words. Words here are simply the tools with which one works. Knowledge is necessarily a priori, since at the very least (with the assumption that the orator is a good man), one needs to know beforehand where one will be leading. The difficulty, however, is deciding if the rhetor needs to know the good and the beautiful, or whether it might be enough to understand what appears to be (259e-261a). The answer, of course, is the former, since to agree to semblance would send the whole of rhetoric back to the flatteries discussed in the *Gorgias*.

Thus Lysias is not a very good rhetor, since to get at any kind of knowledge one must be able to recognize similarities and dissimilarities among things (requiring knowledge), divide and categorize, and ultimately reassemble the parts into a coherent whole. Here Socrates uses the metaphor of the body as a way of considering the whole-ness of something that is nonetheless a composite. Indeed, Kathy Eden points out that for Socrates the part depends on the whole (22). Kenneth Burke calls this the universal appeal of form (*Rhetoric of Motives* 58). We might go further. The whole is precisely that which one should seek knowledge of. This of course jibes with the Platonic notion of forms, which are necessary, pre-given and lie outside of discourse (dialectical or rhetorical). As Susan Handelman puts it, "Through discourse . . . one can formulate the intelligible structure or makeup of a thing (its logos), but this formulation is not identical with the thing itself" (8). That makeup, the limbs and trunk and head, are themselves descriptions of something outside, prior, and immutable. In a different context—that of the Christian Trinity—Burke argues that

> There is a kind of *correspondence* between the thing and the name for the thing. There is a state of *conformity*, or *communion*, between the symbolized and the symbol. Insofar as we are considering merely the relation between a name and the thing it names, some such technical term as "correspondence" or "conformity" will serve out purposes. But insofar as the Trinity is said to be composed of "persons," we must translate our idea of perfect correspondence in to correspondingly personal terms. And the word for perfect communion between *persons* is Love. (*Religion* 29-30)

If Love is the personal name for correspondence between the symbolized and symbol in this case, it is perhaps for similar reasons that Plato, while working out the relation of words qua rhetoric to truth via the relations of and to people, has Socrates spend so much time on the relation of body and soul via the nature of love.

Socrates acknowledges that oratory (rhetoric) is indeed concerned with the soul (*Phaedrus* 217d). When the soul is perfect, says Plato, it is immortal and soars high and is able to behold what Plato calls "true being," the proper condition of the soul before it takes a body. It is to this condition that each soul aspires after it is embodied, to a greater or lesser degree (249a-e). People are mortal, and under consideration here is mortal love as an effect of this embodiment. Plato is making a case for love as an inherent yearning for the prior divine condition. In this sense, if love is not entirely logos, it is at least a condition in which logos blossoms.

People are composites of souls and bodies and their souls yearn for their previous flight. When those mortals who can remember seeing true being (people whose souls remember encountering "true being") see its likeness here on earth, "they are amazed, they are no longer masters of themselves" (250a). According to Plato, the likeness in question is most readily available through the beautiful since beauty is the most manifest evidence of the true (what veritably is) (250d). Then when one sees a bodily form that *expresses* beauty, one is overcome by it. One loves. Two things are important here. The first is that this beauty is an expression of (the likeness or re-presentation of) something else, something that is no longer available to the mortal-who-loves. The second is that the beauty of the beloved is understood as issuing out of the beloved and coming into, possessing the lover who yearns for the immortal, the true, the sublime. The former case is the inherent condition described above; for mortals, the soul is always already missing the true (though it might remember). Its primary condition is that of lack here figured as a loss intrinsic to mortality. To be mortal means to be missing some part of the divine.[11] The second point then indicates a peculiar paradox, since what is fundamentally missing from the lover is recognized in love as issuing from the beloved, at least as a likeness, an image of what is true. That is, the beloved does indeed seem to have access to that part of the divine that is missing from every mortal. The likeness or image covers over a fundamental lack by (apparently) converting an intrinsic condition (that of lacking) into an extrinsic discovery (a positivized *je ne se quoi* in the other). [12]

The presence of the beloved brings a certain amount of joy and satisfaction, while his absence causes pain. When the lover is parted from his beloved, the lover's soul "remembers the boy in his beauty [and] it recovers its joy. From the outlandish mix of these two feelings—pain and joy—comes anguish and helpless raving; in its madness the lover's soul cannot sleep at night or stay put by day; it rushes, yearning, wherever it expects to see the person who has that beauty" (*Phaedrus* 252d-e). The memory here is actually a reminder of (and occasion for the image of) the true being that the soul is always already missing.[13] In addition, the beloved may be understood as the lover's construct or even fantasy insofar as the selection of a beloved is dependent upon the lover's disposition (Zeus-like, Mars-like) and "[e]veryone chooses his love after his own fashion from among those who are beautiful, and then treats the boy like his very own god, building him up and adorning him as an *image* to honor and worship" (252e, my emphasis). Those lovers who are, say, Zeus-like seek after their god in memory—here the memory the soul has from before it became embodied—and emulate him, all the while assuming that this drive toward the divine issues from the beloved and at the same time changing the beloved into the image of their god (253.a-c). What needs to be stressed is that the memory that the soul has *both is and is not* the condition of the embodied soul. As memory, it still marks a fundamental lack in the mortal. We can call the condition loss only by referring to a pure, pre-ontological status of the soul. This pre-ontological condition is, for Plato, "pure fiction, based neither on observation nor on adequate reasoning," thus pushing the argument back to the other side, as it were, to the consideration of images, likenesses, pale imitation (246.c-d).

As far as the beloved is concerned, the beloved receives from the lover what Plato calls a counter-love. The beloved spends time with his lover and the beauty (the flood of passion) flows out of the beloved into the lover. The lover overflows with it. The beloved recaptures this beauty (which has been changed into something else via the lover—into love), and in turn, becomes a kind of lover (255b-e). This new beloved-lover possesses only the image of love, however, since the beloved-lover does not recognize the origin of love himself (though the beloved is already a reflection of the lover's desire for the true). The beloved-lover position or state, then, is a condition similar to that of the primary lover, since the beloved-lover mistakes the intrinsic (lacking) for the extrinsic (positive), too. Then, in the case of the beloved, Plato explicitly points to the economy we suggested above for the lover.

The lover sees in his beloved what he himself has lost: a divinity. What the lover really recognizes in his beloved is the lover's reflected desire for completeness—a reunion with the missing divine. The beloved, the crucible of so much beauty, so much love, radiates that love until the lover becomes so full he overflows with it. Thus the beloved gets the backwash of what he previously sent out. The lover, it appears, is replete; the beloved is lessened.

Is Plato's understanding of the function of the image the same as Longinus's insistence on the sublime as an effect of the image? Plato is concerned with finding (evidence of) divinity in the image of the divine, in beauty. Longinus is also concerned with such divinity when he writes that the figure—figure of speech, but also the figure as correlating to the image—is at its best when it escapes attention (17.1). What Longinus argues for is an art that *seems to be* nature (22.1), thereby allowing a move from imitation to the thing (from written word to spoken, and so on) that Plato strictly forbids. Beauty (and sublimity) is considered by Longinus to be an effect of art, not something in-itself, a "true being." Longinus's concern is less what the soul has forgotten by taking a body and more what, once the soul is embodied, can or will evoke the sublime through the image which allows for a mis-presentation analogous to Plato's. When you present an image, "you seem to see what you describe and bring it vividly before the eyes of your audience" (15.1). This is the same confusion we found in Plato above, but with a twist. In the *Ion*, Socrates claims that a successful performance for the rhapsode is an instance of divine possession and asks Ion, "are you at that time in your right mind, or do you get beside yourself? In its enthusiasm, does your soul believe it is present at the actions you describe . . . ?" Ion agrees: "Listen, when I tell a sad story, my eyes are full of tears; and when I tell a story that is frightening or awful, my hair stands on end with fear and my heart jumps" (535c). The performer—the rhapsode, of course, but we could extend the claim to the rhetor or even author without too much work—in some way participates with the audience. In terms of the *Phaedrus*, the audience is the lover, but so is the performer. Both are in the thrall of the presented image. What is beloved is precisely the (spoken or written) text, from whence the image is misrecognized as originating.

For a contemporary example, consider a scene from Neil LaBute's film *Your Friends and Neighbors* (1998) in which three characters—Barry, Jerry, and Cary (played by Aaron Eckhart, Ben Stiller, and Jason Patric)—discuss their finest sexual experiences. To the other two friends' surprise, the lothario Cary chooses as his "best fuck" the gang rape of Timmy Carter, a high school snitch, in which he participated. We are given a medium long shot of the three of them wrapped in towels, sitting in a steam room with Cary in the middle and slightly above his friends (suggesting teacher-and-students, perhaps). Cut to a medium shot as Cary begins to tell his story, followed by a very slow push to Cary's face as he describes how he was the last of the boys to mount Timmy and that he, Cary, was certain that something "special" happened then, that Timmy "did everything right," how it has "never been like that with a woman," that, though the other boys are holding Timmy spread out, the two of them were "making love on some beach in the Mediterranean," etc. The scene ends with Cary maintaining that the act was special for Timmy, too, that Cary was special for Timmy. That "I just didn't expect to find somebody who, you know, understood me, is all."

Besides the brutality being described, what is even more frightening about the scene is its honesty. Through the slow push of the camera (so slow that one viewer told me she thought at first she was leaning in; that is, participating), it is clear that, as Cary tells the story, he is also (re)experiencing the act. His eyes are unfocussed (or, rather, focused on something far away, a memory), and we-the-audience *see Cary seeing it*. And what Cary conjures for himself is love, is the sublime insofar as love is precisely the substitution/misrecognition of something as the Thing that is missing.

Longinus states: "In literature . . . we look for something greater than the human" (36.3). It is not too much of a stretch to recognize this transcendence as precisely the effect of love Plato argues. So when Plato suggests that writing, like painting, presents only the image of the true thing and is thus a lesser imitation of living speech and so should not be taken seriously, we cannot help but recognize that this is also the love relation Plato describes (*Phaedrus* 275d-e). And does not the beloved represent the image of the lover's god (the god inside the lover which is in some way always already missing) and so love himself, if to a lesser extent, through the image of love? In this sense, the spoken or written of Longinus' formulation may be understood as the beloved (the Timmy?) of its audience. And the author also loves, which allows a particular orientation of the author with the audience (and Socrates' position as a "lover of discourse" or wisdom, a lover of what he himself *seems* to produce).

So as little as Plato thinks of writing as opposed to living speech, we find writing's analog in the love-relation he explicates. Compositions are a means of reminding those who know the truth *just as the beloved reminds the lover of true being* (Longinus 278a). Love is a reminder of the soul's divinity insofar as the lover finds his own missing image (or likeness) in another and (mis)reads this reflection as something outside, mistaking the intrinsic lack for an extrinsic presence-in-appearance. Conversely, written or spoken text for Longinus sets the conditions for the beloved's (the text's) move toward the attitude of lover—the mis-recognition of the extrinsic as intrinsic, what is written or heard as having already been there in the writing.

There are two terms here, writing as an act and the written as that essential, formal aspect of which all writing shares. The conflict (or shift, or mis-recognition) is between the written and the reader, not between the author and audience. And sublimation might then be seen as a condition for the mis-recognition. Love is an action (one loves), but sublimation is the state of *being* (lack) as it is recognized as loss. That is, sublimation is the very context for, the condition of, misrecognition, and the Sublime would be its positivization. One does not sublimate (as one displaces) but is sublimated. The written presents the image of speech (for Plato) in the same way that love presents the image of the divine (as reflection). Longinus moves all of this philosophy into a kind of logology, where we find the sublime in rhetoric insofar as rhetoric relates to the figure qua logos as the intelligible makeup of the thing, its image. And so we may love text, as long as it offers (the occasion for) misrecognition of the truth.

That the truth (of the soul, of the divine) is assumed prior to its enunciation is, well, assumed, and thus is the basis from which any good rhetoric—that is, philosophical rhetoric—must proceed. The process involves a negotiation of hierarchies:

> First, you must know the truth concerning everything you are speaking or writing about; you must learn how to define each thing in itself; and, having defined it, you must know how to divide it into kinds until you reach something indivisible. Second, you must understand the nature of the soul, along the same lines; you must determine which kind of speech is appropriate to each kind of soul, prepare and arrange your speech accordingly, and offer a complex and elaborate speech to a complex and elaborate soul and a simple speech to a simple one. Then, and only then, will you be able to use speech artfully, to the extent that its nature allows it to be used that way, either in order to teach or in order to persuade. (Longinus 277b-c)

That first, of course, is actually second. First, there is truth, and then you must know it. Then you must be able to divide and subdivide it into constituent, more palatable parts. At the same time, you must be able to do the exact same thing with souls. That is, you must know the true nature of the soul that can then be divided into particular kinds that you should be able to address particular kinds of speech or writing. This creates a dual descent from the true. On the one hand, the subject under discussion must be treated scientifically, vivisected and spread out, each organ numbered and weighed. Likewise, the audiences addressed, inasmuch as audiences are composed of souls, should be understood in both their similarities and dissimilarities and treated accordingly.[14] As Kennedy points out, for Plato, "a true 'rhetorician' would do something similar [to dialectic] and there is little logical difference between dialectic, or the discovery of truth, and rhetoric, or the persuasive exposition of truth. Both have the same 'logical structure'" (57). It is evident that the practical priority given to philosophy. First there must be a climb up toward the true (say, the philosopher is a mountaineer and dialectic is his climbing ax), the discovery of parts and their synthesis into what can be said to be immutably so (in order to place the flag on the summit and claim it). Such is philosophy, without which, it seems, there is neither science nor rhetoric.[15] The good rhetorician for Plato is primarily a good philosopher who has knowledge (who has done the philosophical climbing beforehand) and is capable of leading others toward it (thus, Plato as Sherpa).

Truth functions as something out there that should be reached for or as a goal toward which people can be lead. It is an extrinsic and immutable (read necessary) cause demonstrated by an inherent loss (a formal descent) that is both defined and proven by the fact of love. Love, then, is a name for both what we are by definition lacking and for what we want. The difficulty is that Plato begins with lack instead of the realization that the discourse itself both conjures a place for Truth and then displaces it as a formal cause.

II. Cause

In book one of the *Rhetoric*, Aristotle takes as his goal the definition and range of rhetoric. He writes at first that rhetoric is the counterpart of dialectic and, later, that it is a branch of dialectic (1354.1, 1356.1). Rhetoric is a branch of dialectic in part because "the consideration of deductions of all kinds, without distinction, is the business of dialectic," and the enthymeme is rhetoric's particular form of deduction (1355.7). This is fairly clear. The relationship is similar to that expounded by Plato.

The function of rhetoric as the counterpart of dialectic, however, causes some confusion in as much as "the technical study of rhetoric is concerned with the modes of persuasion" and "persuasion is a sort of demonstration" (1355.4-5). Well and good. Rhetoric's "sort of demonstration" is like its form of deduction, which is a branch of dialectic. The difficulty, though, with bringing in (any) forms of demonstration is that demonstration implies some kind of instruction, if only concerning the direction one must go in order to do good things. And it is the job of rhetoricians to persuade people toward the true and just; although Aristotle writes that rhetoricians should be able to apply their skills on both sides of an argument, they "must not make people believe what is wrong" (1355.31). So we can assume that dialectic and rhetoric have the same goal (which makes sense if rhetoric is a part of dialectic), but where dialectic is generally concerned with knowledge derived from induction and deduction, the enthymeme allows for a gloss, a quick way to get the same result. Knowledge, Aristotle writes, "implies instruction, and there are people whom one cannot teach" (1355.26-27). And it is to these people that we must turn our rhetorical acumen. If a house is on fire and a child is inside, one might take the time to explain that we are inside a burning house, that people inside burning houses die horrible deaths, and therefore, we should leave the house toot sweet. But it is much easier (and ultimately safer) to yell out that it's much cooler outside, let's go out for ice cream, and try to keep up.

A further apparent difference between philosophical reasoning and rhetorical display might be rendered in terms of time and action. Though Aristotle's *Rhetoric* assigns times to his three kinds of rhetoric (past, future, and present for judicial, deliberative, and epideictic), we might recognize the formal *presentness* of their object. Though the subject of judicial oration is likely some past event, its goal is to establish what action is just or unjust *now*. Punish or praise, but do it now. So too, with the deliberative, though the actions may affect the future (of the state, the family, whatever) it is the present decision that is addressed through appeal to the future. Perhaps this is why so much of these two forms can be identified in the epideictic, since this last takes present opinion most conspicuously as its object. The rhetorical concern is immediacy and engagement with the world as it is (or, perhaps, as it seems to be). So, whereas the philosophical project is geared toward the discovery or proof of some kind of extratemporal *being*, rhetoric might be understood as a call to action premised on that being. Do something now; here is your motivation.

Regardless, we find that rhetoric is at once part of dialectic (insofar as they both profess to say something about the world) and different from dialectic in terms of its process, or rather, the conditions under which one or the other is appropriate. Kenneth Burke puts this dual understanding of rhetoric another way and so makes an argument for his curve when he writes that:

> since "rhetoric," "oratory," and "eloquence" all come from roots meaning "to speak," you can have the Aristotelian stress

> upon rhetoric as *sheer words*. In this respect, by his scheme, it is the "counterpart" of dialectic.... Some theorists may choose to look upon the rhetorician as a very narrow specialist [which he is if rhetoric is but a branch of dialectic]. On the other hand, since one can be "eloquent" about anything and everything, there are Quintilian's grounds for widening the scope of rhetoric to make it the center of an entire educational system. He was here but extending an emphasis strong in Cicero, who equated the ideal orator with the ideal citizen, the man of universal aptitude, sympathies, and experience. And though Aristotle rigorously divided knowledge into compartments whenever possible, his *Art of Rhetoric* includes much that falls under the separate headings of psychology, ethics, politics, poetics, logic, and history. Indeed, according to him, the characteristically rhetorical statement involves "commonplaces" that lie outside any scientific specialty; and in proportion as the rhetorician deals with special subject matter, his proofs move away from the rhetorical and towards the scientific. (*Rhetoric of Motives* 51)

Burke then continues to argue persuasively for an apparent progression from Aristotle to Augustine, with the latter's emphasis on instruction. Burke is a very good rhetorician. But there is another problem. Burke calls persuasion "the essence and end of rhetoric" (49). This is not, however, exactly what Aristotle says: "Rhetoric may be defined as the faculty of observing in any given case the available means of persuasion" (1355b.27). Rhetoric is the faculty (*dunamis*) of observing the available means of persuasion, not persuasion itself. The obvious question, then, is what is a faculty?

In *The Lost Cause of Rhetoric*, David Metzger wonders what it means when Aristotle writes that rhetoric is a *dunamis*, "given that the word *dunamis* figures prominently in both his *Rhetoric* and his *Metaphysics*" (27). Metzger allows that Aristotle likely understood rhetoric and metaphysics as two distinct kinds of inquiry and that the word *dunamis* may have varied meanings depending on context, but insists that "Aristotle's use of *dunamis* in the *Rhetoric* informs his use of the word in the *Metaphysics*—if only insofar as rhetoric is a thing which does, in fact, exist in the Aristotelian 'system' " (27-28). If we allow this relation between the two texts, then what does it mean to say that rhetoric is a faculty? Precisely that rhetoric "is the presumption, not the assumption, of the possibility of persuasion" (30). That is, rhetoric is to be understood as the ground from which one proceeds and not part of the particular, "historical" context or circumstance. Rhetoric is possibility, pure potential. Rhetoric is logically prior to any given act of persuasion. And this jibes with the definition of *dunamis* Aristotle gives in the *Metaphysics*, which is "the source of motion or change which is in something other than the thing changed, or in it qua other" (1019a). In terms of rhetoric, we might then say that it deals with the *potential* to persuade and that this potential lies outside of rhetoric's subject or within it as something alien.

It is precisely rhetoric as a potential, not a circumstance, which brings us to Aristotle's basic ontological assumption. Aristotle cites Plato's stress in the *Cratylus* on the contingent nature of language to remind us that names are merely an imitation of ideas, which are of course related to the ideal forms. As Susan Handelman points out, "[t]he model for this sort of thinking is at bottom mathematical. So, too, the ideal is a mathematical language abstracted from objects, above contingency; number, not words, provides access to true knowledge of reality" (5). That is, the mathematical avoids the "natural" object in favor of its form. This mathematical understanding is what leads to Aristotle's logic, which has to maintain certain necessary and primary premises which are "didactic, assumed, not questioned" in order to both allow the possibility of "proof" and to indicate how it is that words, which are contingent, may nevertheless have an effect (6). Even if words (especially names) are contingent, there must be something behind them. And this *something behind them* is precisely the *dunamis* Aristotle posits.

But what do we make of this being qua other?

Imagine a room with a floorboard nail sticking up. I want to hammer that nail back in, butI have no hammer. I do, however, have a chair. I can use the leg of that chair to push the nail down and my problem will be solved. Now comes my dilemma. Do I still have a chair, given that I (can) use it as a hammer? Of course I do. The chair does not change, but we might say that its potential as hammer rests in it but as something other than chair: as a hammer. However, a problem arises when we ask ourselves why we should bother having hammers at all; given that here we can use a chair to hammer with the same effect. Suppose that we extend this question further and define the entire world through chair-ness or by various becomings of chair. Enter

Aristotle to save us from such a world. In order to limit the shifting of things made possible by *use*, Aristotle has to posit something that does not change with use—the prime mover that is itself unmoved. That is, this mover is never *used* by something else (there is nothing else above it in this hierarchy) but is the guarantee that there is an end to the shifting, that all things are grounded. There is some other which is primary, necessary as a referent, but which does not shift with use the way a chair can. And this mover is both necessary and *useless* as an inactive source of action. The Useless Mover is precisely the metaphysical god.

Well, sort of. It should be clear that what is established by this hierarchical framework is not a temporal process, but a logical relation. As Burke writes:

> The Aristotelian God . . . acted upon nature neither as creator nor generator, but as a motionless inducement to development. The world and its genera and species were considered as eternal, hence not as derivations from God as "pure act." God acted upon nature solely as a goal, somewhat as a desired food might, by lying west of a rational and hungry man, induce him to move towards the west; or as the principles of a perfect art might lead the knowing artist to shape his work as nearly as possible in accordance with them. (*Grammar* 68)

We can read development as a temporal process; we can tell the story of a man moving west toward food. In this case, narrative functions as an example of logical assumed relations.[16] Whereas ultimates are eternal and motionless and function solely as principles. That is, following Burke's simile, food lying west doesn't do anything; it just is. Action comes in when a "rational and hungry man" moves toward it. And we say that this involves action (that is, motivated movement) rather than simple movement because our man is both rational and hungry. Food lying west does not *cause* movement toward it, hunger does, and more than that, knowledge that the food is indeed west of here. Once again, knowledge is a priori, and in this case, knowledge of a lack of food. So, the principles of a perfect art (whatever that might be) can lead the artist who knows them toward—if not all the way to—them (we should be reminded of Plato's assumption of knowledge, of course, as well as that "within human limits" from his definition of good rhetoric in the *Phaedrus*). These principles, immutable and pre-given, function as a kind of gravity for wise people and, as the potential to persuade is also a principle, allow the possibility of leading the unwise in the right direction, too.

Principles exist prior to any motive, act, or even movement. They simply are, and in this sense *are* ahistorical constants. According to Burke:

> "Principles" are "firsts," but they are "absolute" firsts, not the kind of firsts that require a temporal succession as we go from a first to a second. They just *are*. They have logical, rather than temporal, priority. Hence, to treat of things in terms of their relation to underlying principles is to translate historical sequence into terms of logical sequence (whereby things can "precede" and "follow" one another in a kind of succession that requires no time coordinate).[17] (*Grammar* 73)

Here we might recognize a basic form of reasoning, the "if/then" ratio, as long as we also recognize that beyond the assumption of the "if" is the presumption of those didactic premises Handelman writes of. And the didactic premise of didactic premises, the God-term to which all other terms are ultimately pinned, is the Aristotelian Mover as inactive cause. Burke continues:

> But if a first and a second are related "logically," they are by the same token related "necessarily." For a logical relationship, or principle of being, always was, is, and will be; and what always was, is, and will be, *must* be. Whereby ontology merges the "is," the "must be," and the rational. (*Grammar* 530)

We could think of such a logical relationship as a part-to-whole relationship, whereby the "if" of a statement reduced to its zero degree, a necessary premise, becomes a representative of the whole and the "then" a simple index of it. If all cats are eaters and my pet is a cat, then my cat eats, too. My cat then functions as a representative of the principle "cat." This is clear; a representative indicates the whole set. And I can shift this logical relationship into the temporal sphere. As a rational and loving man, I move toward the cat food. But there is a danger to this kind of shifting. We can imagine a situation when a logical reduction—say, the "all men are mortal" syllogism—could become a rationalization (in the full sense of the word) for homicide or suicide. We will discuss causality and temporality more carefully later. For now, we can return to Burke:

> But if a first and a second are "necessarily" related...we cannot have arbitrariness and magic. Creator (the first) and creature (the second) thus become "coequal and coeval," in being *ontologically* related (that is, *logically* related in terms of *being*). The second is then related to the first somewhat as conclusions are implicit in premises and premises are implicit in conclusions. (*Grammar* 74)

Being guarantees temporality, predication, and the necessary. This is one way of figuring the Christian turn by imagining God and Christ as coeval. But then why do we need both God and Christ for good theology? Why isn't a Mover enough to get the Christianity ball rolling?

III. Augustine's Christianizing

In book four of *On Christian Teaching*, Augustine supplies a kind of reversal of Aristotle's claim that rhetoricians must not make people believe what is wrong by assuming that his readers might object to good (Christian) people learning pagan (bad) rhetoric. Here, Augustine asks "Since rhetoric is used to give conviction to both truth and falsehood, who could dare to maintain truth, which depends on us for its defense, should stand unarmed in the fight against falsehood?" (Augustine and Green 4.4, 101). The effects of this and subsequent statements are several. He calls rhetoric "the rules of eloquence," but the rules seem not to be the *dunamis* Aristotle deals with. Rather, Augustine assumes (rather than presumes) persuasion insofar as he imagines that the use of rhetoric (this is not a rhetoric that uses) is the condition of and for teaching, rather than a way around it.

In other words, Augustine accepts Quintilian's expansion of rhetoric into the sphere of general education (see 4.3, 101) while denying Cicero's equating of eloquence with moral excellence, since good rhetoricians may "give conviction to both truth and falsehood." As Kenneth Burke puts it, "Augustine was pleading for a 'truth' greater than any purely human kind of moral grandeur" (*Rhetoric of Motives* 76). According to Burke, Cicero equates rhetoric with wisdom,

> whereas Augustine is relating them in preferential order. In his scheme, wisdom...is a "source of eloquence," not because

> it is one with eloquence (since the "truth" of Christian doctrine can be stated without eloquence), but because it is the *ground* of eloquence [this is apparent in 4.6]. Thus, whereas Aristotle grouped rhetoric with dialectic by reason of the fact that both were purely verbal instruments, in Augustine...dialectic is more than words: for when it is correct, it deals with the ultimate nature of *things*, hence has a kind of extra verbal reference to guide the use of ornament (eloquence, rhetoric). The end of rhetoric was "to persuade with words"...but the principle of Logos behind such purely human language was "the Word" in another sense, a kind of Word that was *identical with* reality. Such seems to be the assumptions underlying Augustine's theories of rhetoric. And they seem to follow from the stress upon teaching as an "office" of rhetoric. (77)

And the "Word that is identical with reality" is precisely Christ as the literal instantiation of every word of the Bible. Interpretation goes hand-in-hand with teaching, of course, since what is to be taught is precisely knowledge of scripture. And where wisdom is concerned in the dispensing of knowledge, Augustine advises: "For a person who has to speak wisely on matters which he cannot treat eloquently, close adherence to the words of scripture is particularly necessary. The poorer he sees himself to be in his own resources, the richer he must be in those of scripture, using them to confirm what he says in his own words" (Augustine and Green 4.21,105).

So scripture is precisely the Word that Burke posits above as being identical with reality, at least as it marks the instantiation of Christ. Though Book 4 dwells on the rhetorical acumen (or eloquence) apparent in scripture, Augustine takes pains in the previous three books to argue that scripture is not fundamentally rhetorical, but that its "truth" has bearing outside the realm of pure speech. Scripture is above all historical, but with "a twist," as illustrated by the following chapter from Book 1, quoted in full:

> Although the truth itself and the word by which all things were made became flesh so that it could live among us [John 1: 3, 14], notice how the apostle says, "And if we knew Christ according to the flesh, we do not know him in the same way now" [2 Cor. 5: 16]. In fact Christ, who chose to offer himself not only as a possession for those who come to their jour-

ney's end but also as a road for those who come to the beginning of the ways, chose to become flesh. Whence the saying, "God created me at the beginning of his ways" [Prov. 8: 22], so that those who wanted to come could begin from there. The apostle, then, although still walking on the road and following God as he called him to the prize of a higher calling, none the less "forgetting what was behind and straining forward to what lay ahead" [Phil. 3: 14, 13] had already passed beyond the beginning of the ways. In other words, he was not deprived of the one from whom the journey must actually be undertaken and begun by all who long to come to the truth and abide in eternal life. For Christ says, "I am the way, the truth, and the life" [John 14: 6]; that is, "you come by me, you come to me, you abide in me." For when you come to him, you come also to the Father [cf. John 14: 6–11], because God, to whom he is equal, is recognized through his equal, and the spirit binds us and as it were cements us together, so that we can abide in the supreme and unchangeable good. From this it is to be inferred that nothing must detain us on our way, since not even the Lord, at least in his graciously chosen role of being our way, wanted to detain us; rather he wanted us to pass on, not sticking feebly to temporal things—even though they were accepted and endured by him for our salvation—but hastening eagerly through them so that we may achieve progress and success in our journey to the one who has freed our nature from temporal things and set it at the Father's right hand. (1.81-83, 26)

The historicizing move is apparent in "'God created me in the beginning of his ways,' so that those who wanted to come could begin from there." As Christ is the fulfillment of the covenant made with Abraham and is both Isaac and the ram of the binding narrative, so too is he the beginning of a new history, a new journey for believers.

Our twist comes when we realize that Christ is made flesh by God-the-Father, who is himself "the supreme and unchangeable good." It is not difficult to map this God onto Aristotle's Mover who is unmoved, but what do we do with Christ? It seems that Augustine would both eat his cake and have it, since God-the-Father is supreme and unchangeable while God-the-Son is by definition the God who moves. Christ *comes down*, is *made* flesh, and *leads* believers on the path to heaven. And these two Gods are the same, since "because God, to whom he is equal, is recognized through his equal." Thus the binitarianian God is both the mover and the moved, both necessary and useful. So the metaphysical god of Aristotle becomes Augustine's God in history, a God for whom all previous events are signs and to whom all subsequent events refer. We need only look at saints' lives narratives in order to see how this works for martyrological purposes.[18] *Now* becomes predicated on a *then* that rises above its status as an event and becomes a predicative truth following the principle of Logos as that which "always was, is, and will be; and what always was, is, and will be, *must* be." The truth of Christianity is precisely the historically locatable Passion, which at the same time fulfills the promise of what preceded it (the Old Testament, etc.) and figures everything coming after. The Passion is a *cause* in its most efficient, historicized sense. Christ's death and resurrection are the ground, the predicate for the Church. And all of scripture is its story.

Augustine's position might be rendered in our terms as an insistence on the logical necessity of the Passion. We can, I think, begin to see the God-Christ relation as a necessary and logical one, though probably not through a syllogism. As a point of doctrine, Christ is perfect. Christ, according to Augustine, decided to take a fleshly body. He in no way *becomes* the savior of humankind, but always already *is*. That is to say, if we read the first-to-second logical ratio laid out before as a God-to-Christ ratio, then, following Burke's insight, the first and second are coeval. The further twist is evident when we consider causality. The imperfection of a humanity relating to a perfect God might be understood as the cause of Christ's fleshly body and the Passion so that Christ's instantiation is a fulfillment of some promise, the end of a history. And reading the Old Testament typologically makes logical sense, as the conclusion is implicit in the premise. But with the Passion, we have a change in causes (a narrowing of the circumference, Burke would say). The Christian Passion becomes a First Cause, the principle from which everything else issues.[19] But this is a cause that is also the beginning of a temporal succession; it even has bearing on how we date things. The Passion is an act that, far from being simply "food lying west," translates everything previous into allegory and restarts history. The world is reborn under a new set of assumed principles, the fundamental principle of which is the Word that is identical with reality. Teaching and doctrine become merely ways of getting at this principle. And the Bible as a text is the documentation of this transformation, the loaves and fishes that call to men who may not even realize that they are hungry.

IV. Love, the Negative, and Christian Logos

We can approach this bifurcation of God through considerations of the nature of love and negativity via (more) Burke. Allowing for the moment that Christ is the physical manifestation of the Word (Logos), then the Word is the preeminent symbol for the world (since it is for the Word that the world is created). And if humans find themselves lacking in relation to the divine—a Christian position, but also a Platonic one, as we have seen—then the human use of language would be a corollary of the divine instance of the Word such that "[i]f the symbol-using animal approaches nature in terms of symbol-systems (as he inevitably does), then he will inevitably 'transcend' nature to the extent that symbol-systems are essentially different from the realms they symbolize. And these realms will be *necessarily* different, inasmuch as the translation of the *extra-symbolic* into *symbols* is a translation of something into terms of what it is not" (*Rhetoric of Religion* 21-22). To talk of anything (and especially of the divine) is to also indicate what is lacking in either our language for it or in the thing itself so that the *name*—as it ropes in any number of separate *things* under its heading and thus transcends the specific stuff—is a kind of participation with/in the supernatural necessary principle, Logos. Thus, words used to describe the supernatural are not exactly positives, in that they don't really or completely describe their objects. Instead, these words should be treated as analogies or metaphors for what they address and, practically speaking, analogy always includes an ignored "but not really" quality.[20] When we actually try to talk about the divine, Burke elaborates, "we must add: 'By *love* we don't mean such love as people have for one another, for that would be merely human. And by *father* we don't mean father in the literal, legal or naturalistic sense of the term'" (23).

Burke is describing the logological principle that "once the word was translated from the realm of social relationships into the supernaturally tinged realm of relationships between 'God' and man, the etymological conditions were set for a reverse process whereby the *theological* term could in effect be *aestheticized*, as we came to look for 'grace' in a literary style, or in the purely secular behavior of a hostess" (7-8). The result is that "there is a sense in which language is *not* just 'natural', but really *does* add a 'new dimension' to the things of nature (an observation that would be the logological equivalent of the theological statement that grace perfects nature)" (8). Language, then, is borrowed to speak about the supernatural in (imprecise) social terms, but that language is thereby tinged with its supernatural applications so that, when we use this (or any) language, we are evoking at once the secular and the supernatural or showing at the same time how each is both *like* and *unlike* the other. In fact, we might argue that what is meant by the use of the word "secular" only makes sense differentially, in relation to the theological, and that when (in the academy or elsewhere) we make the point that what we are talking about is secular, we mean that precisely in the sense that we're not trying to evoke a theological principle.[21] The point to be made is that this not-theological is in essence a negative theology. Words handle the natural world in much the same way as they describe the supernatural, inadequately in their reduction of the particular under assumed blanket terms and super-adequately as they demonstrate a common share the natural and supernatural have in the symbolic structures that define us a the symbol using animal. In the first case we find a negativity that seems to be intrinsic to language as it is used and in the latter we find the correlation of the natural and supernatural via the tingeing of the secular with the divine. And this correlation, much like the reciprocality of Father and Son, is Love.

If we follow this logic, then the negative is a quality of language and is thus presumed in the act of enunciation. Further, Burke argues:

> The Biblical myth pictures natural things as coming into being through the agency of God's Word; but they can merely do as they were designed to do, whereas with God's permission though not without his resentment, the seed of Adam can do even what it has been explicitly told not to do. The word-using animal not only understands a thou-shalt-not; it can carry the principle of the negative a step further, and answer the thou-shalt-not with a disobedient No. Logologically, the distinction between natural innocence and fallen man hinges about this problem of language and the negative. Eliminate language from nature, and there can be no moral disobedi-

ence. In this sense, moral disobedience is "doctrinal." Like faith, it is grounded in language. (*Rhetoric of Religion* 186)

And the formative negativity of language applies to both the natural world (as it is codified with/in/by language) and to the supernatural (as the divine is not *really* as we characterize it, but is only thus by analogy) so that in both cases what language offers is a version, an image of the thing and this image is ultimately of the Thing, the Word to which ontological being is pinned. That is, the Thing or Word is extrinsic to being while at the same time functions as the condition for the set of everything that can be spoken or written (the symbolic order *tout* court). But while words and the things they re-present are not identical, there is a kind of practical correspondence at the level of the noumenal world that finds its complement in the supernoumenal, where "insofar as the Trinity is said to be composed of 'persons', we must translate our idea of perfect correspondence into correspondingly *personal* terms. And the word for perfect communion between *persons* is 'Love'" (30).

For Burke, the Third Person of the Trinity (Holy Spirit) is Love engendered by the logical reciprocality of the Father and Son:

> Note also that whereas the first moment (the thing) provided the ground for the second moment (the appropriate name), both of these moments, taken together, form the "correspondence" between them. Here again the analogy of the Trinity holds, since the First Person is said to "generate" the Second, whereas the Third proceeds from the First and the Second in their togetherness. That is: The technical *correspondence* between thing and name would have as its theologic analogue the "Love" between the First and Second Persons. (30)

The theological principle analogous to the first and second moments is that, while in purely temporal terms a father precedes a son, we can say that the symbolic position of "father" arrives necessarily from having a "son," so that "father" and "son" are reciprocal and the fact of God is dependent upon his Word being consubstantial with him. Thus:

> The Word is also equatable with God's Will, which likewise is co-eternal with Him, pertaining to His very Substance. By this step, Augustine rounds out his Trinitarian Pattern, and

> thereby asserts that God's Will must not have changed either; God's decision to create the World by His Word could not have "arisen " (*exortum est*), but would be part of the eternal principle. This point would in effect bring the Holy Spirit into the design. (Here, by the way, is a line of thought that, as Spinoza shows, can lead to pantheism. For if a decision to create the world is coeternal with God Himself, then the "principle" of its creation is a "necessary" part of God's nature—and pantheism is technically reducible to the doctrine that the necessary relation between Creation and Creator applies in both directions, Creator needing the Creation as essentially as Creation needs the Creator.) (145)

Burke's parenthetical indicates in what sense Spinoza was a heretic as the latter pushed a point of doctrine to its logical conclusion.[22] As Slavoj Žižek argues, "in order for an ideological edifice to occupy the hegemonic place and legitimize the existing power relations, it HAS [sic] to compromise its founding radical message—and the ultimate 'heretics' are simply those who reject the compromise, sticking to the original message" (*On Belief* 8). Practically, the point made here is that by maintaining the consubstantiality of God and Christ (as Word or Logos), an analog is created by which God seems to depend on his creation in order to be the God of something (as a father must be the father of someone).

This state of affairs allows Žižek to make the further claim that:

> When Saint Augustine opposed Christianity, the religion of Love, to Judaism, the religion of Anxiety, when he conceived of the passage from Judaism to Christianity as the passage from Anxiety to Love, he (again) projected onto Judaism the disavowed founding gesture of Christianity itself—what Christianity endeavors to overcome through the reconciliation in Love is *its own constitutive excess*, the unbearable anxiety opened up by the experience of the impotent God who failed in His work of creation, i.e., to refer again to Hegel, the traumatic experience of how the enigma *of* God is also the enigma *for* God Himself.... (*On Belief* 132)

While we will consider (some of) Judaism in the next chapter and the nature of trauma in the fourth and fifth, if the "reconciliation in Love" for Žižek is something like Burke's formulation of Holy Spirit as the mark or sign of the togetherness of the First and Second Persons, then love of God (and love for one another) would be a participation in that reciprocality, if only partly or imperfectly.

Love, in its strictly Platonic rendering, is what makes up for the fact that we are separated from the divine (since "by 'love' we don't mean such love as people have for one another, for that would be merely human. And by 'father' we don't mean father in the literal, legal or naturalistic sense of the term"). Love is a comfort that covers over the fundamental lack, both the negativity (per Burke) inherent in the introduction of the symbol/symbolized problem and the anxiety engendered by the suspicion that the Creator needs his creation. But, in its Christian formulation, love would also be a potential (*dunamis*) insofar as love is a principle of reconciliation with the divine via, in this case, the Passion as a rhetorical (that is, *present*) act. Graphically, we might render a complicated Christian time-line thusly:

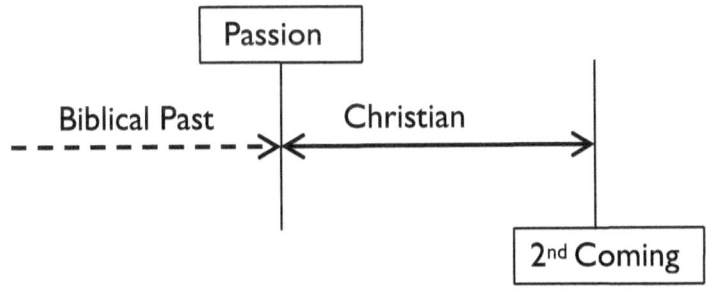

Figure 2. The Christian Present. Illustration by the author.

So that on the one hand the past and present look to the Passion as the event that gives both their meaning and on the other hand the present is moving toward a conclusion implied by its beginning, as the first coming of Christ sets into motion the narrative that will conclude with his return. In a sense, then, Christians' necessary preoccupation with the Passion means that they move toward the second coming backwards, like a happier Angel of History.

As a new cause, the Passion is an act done out of or because of love. And the sacrifice seems to be the taking on of corporeal, temporal form by the divine as much as it is the actual crucifixion. That is, time is restarted via love as an act of God. As Burke writes regarding Augustine's *Confessions*:

> We learn from his own testimony, for instance, that his dreams were not converted. In this sense, the attempted coercing of appetite...still made him a victim of guilt. And the Word took over this victimage, by becoming Mediator in the cathartic sense. In the role of *willing* sacrifice (a sacrifice done through *love*) the Second Person thus became infused with the motive of the Third Person.... Similarly, just as Holy Spirit is pre-eminently identified with the idea of a "Gift," so the sacrificial Son becomes a Gift *sent* by God. (*Religion* 167)

In this economy, Love is the infusion of the Second Person (who is logically consubstantial with the First) with corporality, even with temporality and thereby contingency. The truly loving act—the act that sets Christian time in motion—is not the Passion qua death, but the investment of the Second Person with the *will* to die (out of love) for our potential salvation by covering over the "disobedient No" engendered by language with the corporeal investment of the Word.[23] Thus love is not simply some recognition of the state of falling from perfection (as it is with Plato), but the potential (perhaps indefinitely deferred) of participating wholly with/in that divine state. Again, Burke:

> By this arrangement, the world is 'Christianized' at three strategic spots: The *emergence* of 'time' out of 'eternity' is through the Word as creative; *present* communication between 'time' and 'eternity' is maintained by the Word as Mediatory (in the Logos' role as 'God-man'); and the *return* from 'time' back to 'eternity' is through the Mediatory God-man in the role of sacrificial victim the fruits of Whose sacrifice the believer shares by believing in the teachings of the Word, as spread by the words of Scriptures and Churchmen. (167)

We can now locate the properly rhetorical in its Christian dimension. With the logical introduction of the Word (whereby God is made Father through the fact of the Son), temporality is established and, as it were, a space is opened up for a world in which natural things "can merely do what they are designed to do." The Word-in-the-world (*logos ensarkos*) qua Christ institutes the rhetorical in the *present*-ness of an embodied (and mortal) time that finds its corollary in the possibility of saying No as well as Yes. And the *pure persuasion* of Christian Love promises the potential for return back to the divine (salvation), if only we have faith in the Word (faith being as much a product of language as the negativity it contests). Early in *The Rhetoric of Religion*, Burke notes that such persuasion, in Aristotelian terms, is "'pure' only insofar as a practically 'successful' outcome were precluded. Protestations of love addressed to some ideal 'unattainable' mistress such as Dante's Beatrice would represent a personalized variant of such formality.[24] Viewed from this formal point of view, 'God' represents the principle of an ideal audience" (34). This preclusion of an outcome is precisely the deferment of reconciliation with the divine described above and is also the condition for believing "the teachings of the Word, as spread by the words of Scriptures and Churchmen" that is the other rhetorical truth of Christian doctrine. In fact, this truth (the Word is Love) is exactly what allows for, even requires, the spreading of the gospel via the rhetorical displays of priest and ministers and theologian and missionaries.

Christian Love is what must be disseminated, and it therefore must be codified (or even codex-ified). Daniel Boyarin writes:

> For Augustine…it is the agreement, the consensus, of all Catholic authorities that is the measure of orthodox truth ["an ideological edifice to occupy the hegemonic place and legitimize the existing power relations" per Žižek]. The ecclesiastical writers speak "with one heart, one voice, one faith." It is riveting that Augustine actually imagines this corpus of the writings of the Fathers as both an imaginary council and as a book: "If a synod of bishops were summoned from all over the world, I wonder if that many men of their caliber could easily be assembled. After all, these men did not live at the same time; rather, at different periods of time and in distant places, God sends, as he pleases and as he judges helpful, a few of his faithful ministers who are excellent beyond the many others. And so, you see these men gathered from different times and regions, from the East and from the West, not to a place to which human beings are forced to travel, *but in a book which can travel to them*." (194)

This collection of writings by the Church Fathers seems to share, at least in its Augustinian treatment, something in common with the polysemous text we will discuss as the Oral Torah in the next chapter. Here, sages from different times speak together in conversation. Still, with the Christian text is a *univocal* interpretation and teaching of scripture—pinned as such teaching must be to an extrinsic cause now split into two—to set against our rabbinic counter-example.

2 Rhetoric as Mitzvah

> *Hence we learn that fear leads to Scripture, Scripture leads to Targum, Targum leads to Mishna, Mishna leads to Talmud, Talmud leads to performance, performance leads to reverence.*
>
> —Sifre Deuteronomy

In the *Confessions*, Augustine reads God's injunction to "be fruitful and multiply" as a call from God to "give us range and opportunity to express in different ways what we understand to be a single truth, and to understand in different ways what we read in a single obscure expression" (Augustine and Wills 342). Augustine's *different ways* and *understanding* seem to be promises of an explicitly open text, but we would do better to focus on the end of the statement, the "single obscure expression."

Augustine is not recommending the famous rabbinic synchronic, polysemous reading of Torah that often ignores strictly contextual meaning in favor of elaborate connections and halakic (legal, practical) prescription. In his introduction to *Midrash and Theory*, David Stern reminds us that Augustine's multiple interpretations are not really the result of engaging a polysemous text, but are rather the

> result of the biblical author's own obscurity. That obscurity may possess divine sanction, but its presence nonetheless creates a hermeneutical dilemma for the biblical exegete, making it impossible for him or her to determine the originally intended meaning of a verse, and thereby leading the interpreter to invent other readings. For Augustine, however, this eventuality is not inherently dangerous so long as those other meanings represent the "truth" and are "congruous with the truth taught in other passages of the Whole Scripture." (25)

That truth is also, of course, the truth we discussed earlier. The Bible is about something, and that something is God and his instantiation in history as Christ (as logos-Love). We have only to unravel its often obscure passages to come at the truth of the Passion as the foundation for the faith. So, there may be a number of interpretations because of some divinely sanctioned obscurity, and these interpretations, even if mutually exclusive, would share in the spirit of the meaning.

Such an understanding relates directly to the split between word and thing in both Plato and Aristotle. But where Plato and Aristotle both find it sufficient to place a prime mover outside of time, Augustine must take Christ into account. Thus, as Susan Handelman puts it:

> The only solution for the gap between word and thing is the incarnation, which thereby provides "unmediated vision," a mode far more attractive than the mediations of the text. The assumption is that the single word is superior to any multivocity of words. Hence the only important signs, as Augustine conceives them, are, inevitably, the sacraments—signs literally become flesh. (118)

That is, where the Greek logos—as "the intelligible structure or makeup of a thing" —was a statement of the "what is" of a thing, its essence or primary being, it was only a statement and not the thing itself (8). The Christian innovation is making the word literally flesh. Not all words, of course, but the Logos that *is* reality, thus privileging the ontological over the temporal (as the Greeks did), but then moving the whole Thing back into history as a (or the) cause. As we saw with Plato, this descent from the logical is properly rhetorical. And, as with the Aristotelian presentness (the three kinds of rhetoric have to do with calls to action *now*), the Christian Passion is both a historically locatable event and is always right now (much in the way transubstantiation works). Thus, the Passion functions both as principle (a logical first or cause) and a temporal, motivated, efficient and/or final cause. All things are subsumed by the literalizing of logos *cum* Logos.

This understanding of scripture as having a single, though often obscure, meaning is very different from rabbinic polysemy. On their position, the rabbinic sources are a little confusing. The Babylonian Talmud cites a stance attributed to the School of Rabbi Ishmael: "And like a hammer that breaketh the rock in pieces, just as a hammer is divided into many sparks, so every single word that went forth from the Holy One, blessed be He, split up into seventy languages" (*Soncino Talmud*. Mas. Shabbath 88b). Besides the coincidental hammer (which is not a chair), this way of reading is something quite different from what we have seen. The word of the Lord, the Torah, is like fire and like a hammer. So what is the rock? We might guess, of course, that the rock is the world (or maybe the people), but the passage is unclear. What is clear is that sparks are produced when the rock is hit so that from one hammer (the Torah), as it strikes against whatever we decide to read as the rock, comes many meanings, many sparks.

The Babylonian Talmud is a little more explicit in tractate *Chagigah*. After quoting Ecclesiastes 12:11 ("The sayings of the wise are like goads, like nails fixed in prodding sticks. They were given by one Shepherd.") and explicating the first part of the verse, Rabbi Yehoshua turns to the wise:

> "The masters of assemblies": these are the disciples of the wise, who sit in manifold assemblies and occupy themselves with the Torah, some pronouncing unclean and others pronouncing clean, some prohibiting and others permitting, some disqualifying and others declaring fit.
>
> Should a man say: How in these circumstances shall I learn Torah? Therefore the text says: "All of them are given from one Shepherd." One God gave them; one leader uttered them from the mouth of the Lord of all creation, blessed be He; for it is written: "And God spoke all these words." (*Soncino Talmud* Chagigah 3b)

Certainly, this passage needs close reading, since the issues at hand seem to be most directly concerned with legal questions, decisions which have to be made in order for the people to act appropriately, and not general exegesis. These issues are crucial for behavior *right now*. The implicit question is "How do we know what to do, given that the rabbis' interpretations and pronouncements can differ?" However, the explicit question is "How then shall I learn Torah?" Superficially, the two questions do not correspond, since the former is concerned with which legal pronouncement to follow and the latter wonders about direct engagement with the text. What seems to happen is the conflation of the two. *What the rabbis say is in some way the same as what the Torah gives.* The conflicting opinions may be read as the sparks in the previous example, inasmuch as they support a particular assumption about the rabbis' position regarding Torah. What the rabbis say is the same as Torah, even in contradiction, since "God spoke all these words." It is possible, then, for rabbis to disagree on the issues and still all be right (as opposed to the Augustinian premise that one might get close enough). But though it seems that this should have caused much confusion, in practice it did not; the lesson is not the univocity of the written text but of the community (of rabbis). The other topic addressed here—one that closely connects with Augustine—is how one might teach and learn, given the promulgation of meanings inherent to such an approach.

There are, we are told, two Torahs: the oral and the written. There is a story in the Babylonian Talmud in which a convert comes to Hillel and asks to be made a proselyte on the condition that he is taught only the written Torah, not the oral. Hillel takes him as a student and teaches him the first four letters of Hebrew (*alef, beth, gimmel, daleth*) and "the following day he reversed [them] to him. 'But yesterday you did not teach them to me thus,' he protested. 'Must you then not rely upon me? Then rely upon me with respect to the Oral [Torah] too'" (Shabbath 31a). We are not told whether Hillel reversed the written forms of the letters or the spoken, but in either case, the intent is clear. The oral is, practically speaking, primary to understanding the written. While the written text may, in fact, exist before it is read and studied, understanding is a product of Oral Torah qua instruction. Put more simply, in order to access the written text in any meaningful way, you have to be taught how to do it.

This is good news for those of us who teach. The simple lesson, it seems, is that "primary" texts can only get one so far; reading the textbook but not coming to class won't cut it. There is something essential about instruction that is not in the textbook. Indeed, the very notion of a "primary text" is troubled as rabbinic culture becomes the dominant voice of Jewish practice in the early centuries of the common era, and these rabbis' notions of what a text *is* shapes the transmission of knowledge into a continual practice, something much more practical than any exercise in finding the "true" meaning.

That is, the kind of process that the rabbis of the late antique promote and, to a certain extent, embody *is Torah* insofar as the processes for discovering (uncovering, generating) knowledge is actually the product, too. Torah is both written and oral; both forms are essential.

The Oral Torah—the collected wisdom of the sages—temporally happens after the written texts the sages are ostensibly commenting on, but is at the same time always *necessarily and practically* prior in order to approach the text. The explicit claim is that the oral (as a hermeneutics, as a practice, even as a response) precedes the written *logically*, since approaching the written text is impossible except through methods in which one is instructed.

The rabbis provide a way out of this temporal difficulty by insisting that the oral and written Torahs are concurrent, that both were given to Moses at Sinai. The reason why one is written and the other is oral (and there are many injunctions to keep them as separate as possible) is given in the homiletic *Pesikta Rabbati* thus:

> Moses asked that the Mishnah also be in written form, like the Torah. But the Holy One, blessed be He, foresaw that the nations would get to translate the Torah, and reading it, say, in Greek, would declare: "We are Israel; we are the children of the Lord." And Israel would declare: "We are the children of the Lord." The scales would appear to be balanced between both claims, but then the Holy One, blessed be He, will say to the nations: "What are you claiming, that you are My children? I have no way of knowing other than that My child is he who possesses My secret lore." The nations will ask: "What is Thy secret lore?" God will reply: "It is the Mishnah." (Piska 5)

So, the oral is contemporary with the written; it is not only the way to read the written text with understanding, but is also the practical proof that the people are, indeed, the People. Anyone—Christians, even atheists—can have access to the written Torah and even read it, so the oral is the tie-breaker. There is clearly a polemical aspect to this position, since it would explicitly deny other groups the same privilege. And insistence on temporal concurrence and the logical priority of the oral tradition assures rabbinic involvement in almost every Jewish cultural matter and shores up rabbinic power. In fact, Daniel Boyarin concludes that "disagreement itself, or at any rate the appearance of disagreement to humans, is exemplary of the divine mind. Instead of conducing to an idea of *homonoia*, the Babylonian Talmud leads to an idea of *polynoia*, the many-mindedness, as it were, of God" (162). Of course, the many minds in fact belong to many rabbis. It might be said, though, that the goal of this notion of Torah is that those who are

Jewish will always be kept talking, and it is this practice of disagreement that maintains the community.

Regardless, the polynoid text is quite different from Augustine's historicizing of God through his Word. Whereas Augustine would align scripture with historical instantiation (Christ) in communion with a new version of the Aristotelian prime mover (God-the-Father), the rabbinic move is to place the burden of substantiation on scripture itself. In the midrash to the first chapter of Genesis, the Torah itself declares, "I was the instrument that the Holy One, blessed be He, used when He practiced His craft.... The Holy One, blessed be He, looked into the Torah and created the world" (*Midrash Rabbah: Genesis* Bereshith I.1). God used the Torah (both written and oral) as a blueprint or guide for the creation of the world. Compare this understanding of Torah with Augustine's understanding of Christ, and we can see where we are heading. In the rabbinic case, scripture is not so much the word of God (or his Son) as much as it is consubstantial with him. Stern explains:

> Although the Torah is described here as though it existed before the creation of the world, like the Logos, the idea is not necessarily Platonic.... the Torah is conceived as the instrument God used in creating the world...which He looks into the way an architect looks into a blueprint, or the way the Rabbis themselves looked into the Torah as the blueprint for the existence they constructed for themselves. Torah, then, is not identical with God; its relationship with him is, one might say, metonymic rather than metaphoric, a matter of existence rather that resemblance. The study of Torah, the activity of midrash, does not constitute an act of directly interpreting God as though the text itself were literally divine. (28)

Torah is not in the same situation, then, as the Second or Third Person we discussed in the previous chapter because it is not identical with (or even a part of) God. What such a stance, in effect, allows is a way out of the difficult nature of God that Augustine must sustain as a God in—but at the same time not of—history. If scripture is indeed God's word, is divine, then Augustine must assume a particular meaning, a "truth," which can be transmitted through careful study and instruction. Such a truth is *necessary*. And this truth is the truth of history as such, the truth of (the certainty of) the Passion, or the truth of Logos *cum* Love. Christ is the way to God (while at the same time being God), and the study of scripture is the study of Christ. But if one splits scripture—the Oral and the Written—then perhaps there is no need to split deities.

Returning to thoughts of causation for a moment, we can approach this a little differently. Kenneth Burke proposes:

> In Aristotle's classification of cause, either a first mover (person, agent) or a last mover (implement, tool, agency) can be classed as an efficient cause. And means are considered in terms of ends. But once you play down the concept of final cause...the distinction between agent and agency becomes sharp. Also, there is a reversal of causal ancestry—and whereas means were treated in terms of ends, ends become treated in terms of means. (*Grammar* 276)

We can readily find analogs to the kind of causation in Augustine's treatment, where the first is God-the-Father (or Christ after the Passion) and the last is the Passion itself, perhaps, or simply Christ as logical necessity. And subsequent history might be read as means pointing back to, reifying, an already established ends (as the return of Christ is the final cause or goal only because he came and died already; the real end has both already occurred and is suspended). Or, as we have seen, agent and agency become coeval. But, "once you play down the concept of final cause," once you all but remove God as an ultimate, first mover (Written Torah) and last mover (the Oral) take on very different statuses.[25]

I should admit here that Burke is offering a critique of capitalism. His example is that, "because there are cars, some men learn to become automobile mechanics, their conception of life purpose deriving from the nature of the instrument which they would service." The point is that such men maintain the status quo. Thus, cars can be viewed as the result of a "life purpose," once we downplay the advent of the first car. Our point is that we can push this further. Such men may not simply maintain, but innovate. Excusing a prior, perfect model from consideration, we make new and different cars: minivans, electric carts, hybrids, diesel trucks, motorcycles, etc. And this proliferation is not simply maintenance, but expansion.

Of course, the rabbis are not concerned with cars. For our purposes, the analogy is faulty, since what is at stake is not the maintenance or innovation of some product (which can be bought, traded, sold), but the constant recreation of the world through the proliferation of text(s). Thus, education qua learning how to read becomes a life purpose.

I. Time and the Text

Preoccupation with what matters *right now*, with issues of practice (and the practical) is what I would call the properly rhetorical dimension of rabbinical texts. If philosophy is concerned with the necessary and the true, rhetoric is concerned with contingency and with the present. Again, Aristotle indicates as much since, though he assigns "times" to the different kinds of rhetoric (the forensic, epideictic, and deliberative), in each case both the rhetorical call and the audience reaction to it are located in the present.

We find evidence of the rabbinic understanding of the people's relation to time qua history in Genesis Rabbah. On verse three of Chapter XVIII, ("My Lord, if now I have found favor in Thy sight."), R. Hiyya taught:

> He said this to the greatest of them, viz. Michael. Let now a little water be fetched (XIII, 4). God said to Abraham, "Thou hast said, 'Let now a little water be fetched.' I swear I will repay thy children (in the wilderness, in inhabited country [the Land—Eretz Israel], and in the Messianic future). Thus it is written, *Then sang Israel this song! Spring up, O well—sing ye unto it* (Num. XXI, 7)—that was in the wilderness. Where do we find it in the Land [sc. Eretz Israel]? *A land of brooks of water* (Deut. VIII, 7). And in the Messianic Future? And it shall come to pass in that day, that living waters shall go out of Jerusalem (Zech. XIV, 8). (*Midrash Rabbah: Genesis* Vayera XLVIII.10)

The passage continues to give further, different examples. We should notice immediately that no mention is made of the (rabbinic) present. The implication is that God's promise does not apply to their situation (diasporic; after the destruction of the second temple). That is, though the promise addresses three points in time for the people, the first two are in the past and the last refers to the future. What should we make of this? Perhaps that the rabbis read God as *absent now*, at least in terms of the covenant he made with them. Such a reading does seem to jibe with R. Hiyya's understanding, insofar as the first two examples have to do with the formation of the people, with establishing them as chosen and moving them into the chosen land, and the last with the reestablishing of the covenant. The point here is that both the past and the future are accounted for. They are taken care of by God. But for the present there is no guarantee.

Slavoj Žižek is thus half-mistaken when he argues that when "Jews wait for the arrival of their Messiah, their attitude is one of suspended attention directed towards the future, while, for Christian believer, *the Messiah is already here*, the event has already taken place" (*Belief* 126). His characterization of the Christian situation seems on target, but the rabbinic point is that the past and the future are correlates. They are *both* taken care of. The result is a bracketing of both ends—the biblical past and the messianic future—from the vast present that is the real object of rabbinic practice:

[——Biblical Past——] ---Rabbinic Present-- [——Messianic Future——]

Figure 3. The Rabbinic Present. Illustration by the author.

Perhaps the rabbis' project might be a present time that runs concurrent with linear,[26] proceeding "history" as an instance of the text that resembles what Baudrillard describes in terms of virtual memory as a "hypertelic memory which stores all data in a constant state of instant retrievability, excluding any work of mourning, any resolution of the past. . . . It knows neither past nor forgetting, is neither archaic nor archaeological. It is, indeed, on the contrary, a perpetual present, an instantaneousness of all psychic events, which show on its surface in a continual, potential *passage à l'acte*" (73). Perhaps the Torahs are this hypertelic memory, and it is in terms of the act as that which is always (potentially) present that we should consider the (rhetorical) practice of being Jewish, insofar as every movement may take on the status of an act. In contrast, the Christian attitude would look very different; God's real and direct involvement with the world begins *anno Domini* (to which all things refer) and ends with the Second Coming (to which the beginning refers).

Sharon Crowley makes the same point in her discussion of contemporary American Christian dispensationalism. Dispensationalists,[27] she claims,

> date the beginning of the present, historical age from Christ's death and resurrection...[forcing] prophecy interpreters to give primacy to the Pauline texts rather than the Gospels, producing what Bruce Bower calls a "Church of Law" rather than a "Church of Love." That is, reliance on Paul rather than Christ shifts the tone, if not the substance, of Christian belief away from love and onto proscription. The result of this shift, according to Boone, is that "the main significance of Christ is to be found in the act of his death" rather than in the truth of his teachings.[28]. . . Dispensationalism renders Christ's teachings as a sideline to its determination of the main act: his triumphant and violent return to Earth. (131)

The result is an understanding of time that superficially resembles the rabbinic notion I am stressing here, but that is not practically the same. According to Crowley, contemporary apocalyptics functionally treat the death of Christ as the catalyst (or switch) that sets into motion the current narrative that finds its climax in the apocalypse. Doing God's work is thus imagined as preparing the way for the kingdom's establishment on earth. In terms of causes, Christ's investiture shifts from its position as a formal cause to his death as efficient cause, which is then conflated with the final cause (with the confusion of means and ends such a move facilitates). This is similar to the causal shifting discussed in the previous chapter, but with the apparently apocalyptic emphasis on the violent return of Christ as the climax that all but replaces Love-Logos with a bloody end.

The rabbinic position is that God is no longer active, in that the rabbis imagine a withdrawal of God from the world which opens up the possibility of history as that which is not or cannot be accounted for, as trauma.[29] The question is not *how can we help God accomplish his goals?* but *what can/should we do in his absence?* That is, the rabbinic situation is not a narrative one—looking both back and forward for a cause-effect ratio, as when Christ begins a chain of events—but an insistence on the *present*-ness of practice, on the preservation of a people. History has no goal. History is not a/the story.

Regarding this chain of events, Žižek is right to maintain that for Christians the Passion is an act by God that begins something new:

> Far from providing the conclusive dot on the *i*, the divine act stands, rather, for the openness of a New Beginning, and it is up to humanity to live up to it. It is as in Predestination, which condemns us to frantic activity: the Event is a pure-empty sign,[30] and we have to work to generate its meaning. "The Messiah is here"—this summarizes the terrible risk of Revelation: what "Revelation" means is that God took upon Himself the risk of putting everything at stake, of fully "existentially engaging Himself" by, as it were, stepping into His own picture, becoming part of creation, exposing Himself to the utter contingency of existence. (*Puppet* 136)

What Žižek in effect argues here is that God himself is the psychoanalytic split subject ($) in relation to an Other that is humanity. And perhaps this splitting is what allows for the binitarian aspect of God (as both Father and Son, First and Second Person).[31] By bending himself to creation, God assumes a limitation inasmuch as he is left open to the contingency of existence, as "we are formally redeemed, subsumed under Redemption, and we have to engage in the difficult work of actualizing it" (137). That is, we must all help God. It is to the work of actualizing that, after Christ, Christians must put their shoulders. Hence, beautiful ceremonies and art and kindnesses, but also crusades. And it may be anxiety over this limit that focuses contemporary dispensationalism on the death of Christ over the teaching of Christ that Crowley indicates, and why this focus appears (from the outside) so manic, so unreasonable.[32] Non-Christians may functionally reveal God's lack, which is intolerable. In fact, the anxiety marks a gap that provokes action literally *for God*, so that he is not revealed as the bifurcated subject he must be if he is to find a place in the physical world and its (hi)story.

By contrast, the rabbis deny the existential investment of/by God. Daniel Boyarin takes up this issue in his reading of Justin Martyr's *Dialogue with Trypho*, where he demonstrates that Justin equates Christ with Logos, thereby arguing for a distinct person consubstantial with God.[33] Though Justin is offering the argument of a distinct person as an answer to those who believed that Old Testament *Angel*, *Glory*, and *Word* are earthly versions or aspects of God, the same argument could be made against rabbinic Judaism, which also rejects the distinct persons. Therefore, the *Dialogue* "articulates Christian identity as theological. Christians are those people who believe in the Logos; Jews cannot, then, believe in the Logos" (39). Justin's project, it seems, is to equate Judaism with Christian heresy, excising both from the Orthodoxy. This is important because, as Boyarin argues, until the end of the fourth century,

> Judaism and Christianity were phenomenologically indistinguishable as entities, not merely in the conventionally accepted sense, that Christianity was Judaism, but also in the sense that differences that were in the fullness of time to constitute the very basis for the distinction between the "two religions" ran through and not between the nascent groups of Jesus-following Jews and Jews who did not follow Jesus. Thus, one of the most characteristic differences between Judaism and Christianity as we know them is the belief in or denial of complexity within the godhead, but in these early centuries there were non-Christian Jews who believed in God's Word, Wisdom, or even Son as a "second God," while there were believers in Jesus who insisted that the three persons of the Trinity were only names for different manifestations of one person. (89-90)

Boyarin' claim—and it is a compelling one—is that rabbinic orthodoxy (that kind of Judaism that eventually becomes hegemonic) is a result of the obverse move Justin makes. This means, then, that rabbinic Oral Torah is self-interested insofar as its redaction does not represent merely a repository of Jewish tradition but is also a way to bolster rabbinic ascendancy by denying the possibility of *two powers in heaven* which is the very foundation of Christianity.

II. The Ascendancy of Torah

Daniel Boyarin's arguments for a relatively late rabbinic orthodoxy that developed against a contemporaneous Christian one is not without problems. Steven Fraade, for one, makes a compelling argument against rabbinic polysemy developing so late, working to demonstrate instead that earlier, less canonical texts offer evidence of these sorts of hermeneutic practices. While Fraade grants that there must have been influences to the rabbinic tradition, it is a mistake to target the late antique, post-Nicaean time period for the new establishment of polysemic hermeneutics via redaction, etc. Fraade asks:

> Must we necessarily historicize this development, attributing it, as Boyarin does, to a fifth- to sixth-century finalization of the split between "rabbinic Judaism" and "orthodox Christianity and the internal exclusion of each one's internal "others" or to the establishment of the post-amoraic Babylonian academies (the two being neither contemporaneous not [sic] geographically proximate to one another) rather than to the thematic and narrative maturation of such traditions in the ongoing course of their transmission? Might such a development be reflective of the degree to which narrativity, in general, is much more pronounced and developed in the Babylonian Talmud than in its Palestinian antecedent, as is the case in later *midrashim* compared to their midrashic antecedents? (38)

Maybe we do not need to historicize in the way that Fraade's Boyarin does. It is true, though, that I find Boyarin's account very compelling. But perhaps it is compelling precisely because it is an *account*. At the very least, the text(s) to which Boyarin refers mark, in Fraade's words, a time in which "narrativity, in general, is much more pronounced and developed." Some functions of narrative will be discussed later, in the third and especially the fourth chapters, but that narrative bubbles up so in the disagreement here makes it noteworthy now. It may be that narrativity allows for the hermeneutics of the later rabbis (or maybe any hermeneutics) to rise to the level of a recognizable program such that, even if Boyarin is incorrect in part or whole (and I am still convinced of neither), the fact that narrativity develops to the extent it does at this point is likely not an accident in a vacuum (Fraade agrees, too[34]), but possibly the result of the kind of dialectic Boyarin describes, so that Boyarin's arguments are functionally accurate even disregarding the historicizing Fraade objects to.

Regardless, returning to the *two powers in heaven* problem, it is worth walking through Boyarin's argument somewhat in order to get at the precise manner in which the rabbis are able to avoid (functionally at least, even if they don't do it on purpose) the separate, coeval Logos.

Boyarin turns to one of the foundational texts for orthodox Christianity, the Johannine Prologue, and treats it as a Jewish midrash, the formal characteristics of which is often

> a homily on a periscope, or extract from the Pentateuch that invokes, explicitly or implicitly, texts from either the Prophets or the Hagiographa as the intertextual framework of ideas and language that is used to interpret or expand the Pentateuchal text being preached. This hermeneutical practice is founded on a theological notion of the oneness of Scripture as a self-interpreting text, especially on the notion that the latter books are forms of interpretation of the Five Books of Moses. That is, it is a scriptural, indeed, an interscriptual practice. Gaps are not filled with philosophical ideas but with allusions to or citations of other texts. (95)

According to Boyarin (following Nicola Denzey), the text being preached in the Prologue is Genesis 1. Thus, the *beginning* in the first verse of John ("in the beginning was the Word") is easily both a reference to and comment on the first verse of Genesis ("In the beginning God created the heaven and the earth") and that the *Word* "was in the beginning with God" is related to Proverbs 8:30 ("Then I was with him as a confidant") and to the Wisdom of Solomon 9:9 ("With you is wisdom, she who knows your works and was present when you made the world"),[35] thus indicating a sliding between Logos and Wisdom that suggest "a pre-Christian world of ideas in which Wisdom was personified and characterized in ways that are very similar to the Logos of Logos theology. [The Wisdom hymns] thus offer evidence that the [beginning of the Prologue] is not a specifically or exclusively Christian product, but a common 'Jewish' theologoumenon, or theological conception, which was later identified with Christ" (97).[36] If Boyarin is correct, then it is possible that John is relying on an inherited text and it is clear that later rabbinic denials of two powers are directed as much at other Jews as they are against Christians (this is the same way that Justin's heresiology works). What is important for our discussion is that Boyarin is insisting that what is posited before Christ's appearance in verse 14—the Logos *Ensarkos*, Logos Incarnate—is Logos *Asarkos*. In fact, in his reading we find Wisdom's three attempts to enter into the world: with Abraham (Genesis 15:1 "the Word of the

Lord came to Abraham in a vision"), with the Torah given to Moses at Sinai, and finally with Christ as Logos Incarnate. Ultimately, then:

> John's typology of Torah and Logos Incarnate is more easily read within the context of what Jacques Derrida has argued is a prevailing assumption of Western thought: that oral teaching is more authentic and transparent than written texts.[37] God thus first tried the text, and then sent his voice, incarnated in the voice of Jesus. After the Prologue, which truly introduces the narrative of the Word's coming into the world, its prehistory and its necessity, the Gospel moves naturally into the main Gospel narration, with a Christology informed at all points by the prehistoric, cosmic myth of the prologue. (Boyarin 104)

The Logos Ensarkos is a better teacher than the Logos Asarkos, thus designating what Žižek calls "a new collective [of believers] held together not by a Master-Signifier [the Law], but by fidelity to a cause [actualizing Redemption]" (*Puppet* 130). And the rabbis must refuse this answer by first denying a second power in heaven. Thus the *Genesis Rabbah*, which has Torah proclaim itself as the blueprint for creation, also maintains:

> R. Isaac commenced with, *The beginning of Thy word is truth; and all Thy righteous ordinance endureth for ever* (Ps. CXIX, 160). Said R. Isaac: From the very commencement of the world's creation, *'The beginning of Thy word is truth.'* Thus, IN THE BEGINNING GOD CREATED [corroborates this statement,] *But the Lord God is the true God* (Jer. X, 10). Therefore *'And all Thy righteous ordinance endureth for ever'* (Ps. loc. cit.). For in regard to every single decree which Thou dost promulgate concerning Thy creatures, they affirm the righteousness of Thy judgment and accept it with faith. And no person can dispute and maintain that two powers gave the Torah or two powers created the world. For *'And* the Gods *spake'* is not written here, but, *And God spake all the words* (Ex. XX, 1); *In the beginning* the Gods *created is not written here*, but IN THE BEGINNING GOD CREATED. (*Midrash Rabbah: Genesis* Bereshith 1,7)

The word of God is not an equal separate entity, is not the Word. Of course, by denying the incarnation, the rabbis are also denying an invested God *now*. Or, rather, they dismiss the trajectory of history—the Christian narrative of completion or goal, so that the current era is in fact a great parenthesis (see Figure 3 above)—in favor of a contingent present that is missing the guarantee of a substantive Logos.

The practical question raised by the rabbinic position, then, is *If God has not promised his help* in the now, *how can there continue to be a people?* This is precisely the question the rabbis take up. What else is left, if not Torah? Certainly, it is in some sense the words of God and therefore a connection with him. But it is something else besides. Torah is the consubstantial blueprint for the world, even the present one. And it is through the study of this particular text that the people are defined, or rather through its study and the actual keeping of its commandments. And this becomes the work of the rabbis. The Torah tells us what to do as long as we know how to read it. And with the advent of Oral Torah, that last *knowing how*, things become clearer and we know how to behave now.[38]

Oral Torah allows God's people to found a place in the world and offers a tradition by which to define themselves in terms of the covenant. But neither the Oral nor Written Torah functions as a genealogy of the faith insofar as all Written Torah may be (and should be) read by the rabbis as happening at the same time, not as narrative at all. On this basis, one can pull various intertexts from the text, since context in the particular always includes the greater context, that of the completeness of Torah. We should read this as the contrary position to the classical mathematical one. Where abstraction leads to truth for the Greeks, the rabbinic mode prefers the specific which then has bearing on the general, on the present. Hence the seeming obsessive rabbinic speculation at the level of the letter, never mind the word. Given that every part of the Torah should be considered equally important, for the rabbis God really is in the details. And Oral Torah, both the means and activity by which one may come to terms with the meanings of scripture, is also the instrument by which the rabbis elaborate their place in the scheme. They create a text *of history*, in the sense that living Torah is the instrument by which one addresses the absent cause on a day-to-day basis. Again, this is not a genealogy *per se*, since rabbis separated by centuries are often presented as having a conversation. Handelman argues:

> The Rabbinic world is, to use a contemporary term, one of *intertextuality*. Texts echo, interact, and interpenetrate. In the

world of the text, rigid temporal and spatial distinctions collapse. The elements of the text are treated as much as objective reality for its students as empirical facts are by scientific observers. The Talmud student of today engages in a debate between Hillel and Shammai (teachers of the first century) as if they were his contemporaries, checks the opinion of another Rabbi from the seventeenth century in support of one side, and draws his own conclusions. (47)

Masters and students engage in the study of Torah (written and oral) as scientists might study the sensible world. In contrast to the "existential engaging" of God discussed by Žižek and described by John as the beginning of a new dispensation (of proving God's efficacy), "Hebraic time is an epistemological mode. Inevitably, the Jews are a people of *history*, of time—wanderers in space, exiled from place, but rooted in time, a time in which linear chronology is overcome by contemporaneity" (37). Indeed, it is the study itself that matters most. Study is the best kind of worship. But neither of these Torahs is God (mover or moved). They are something else.

The Talmud tractate *Baba Mezia* relates a dispute among rabbis pertaining to issues of what is clean and what is not. R. Eliezer is apparently the only holdout on the particular point being argued, and we are told that he brings forth every imaginable argument for his position. When these do not work, he calls to heaven for signs that he is correct. A carob-tree is uprooted and moved, water flows upstream, and walls bend in as if to fall. Finally, a Heavenly Voice cries out:

> "Why do ye dispute with R. Eliezer, seeing that in all matters the halachah agrees with him!" But R. Joshua arose and exclaimed: *"It is not in heaven"* (Deuteronomy 30:12)....the Torah had already been given at Mount Sinai; we pay no attention to a Heavenly Voice, because Thou hast long since written the Torah at Mount Sinai, *After the majority must one incline* (Exodus 23:2). (Baba Mezia 59b)

What is immediately apparent is that, in this case and in many others, the truth of a particular instance is decided upon (that is, interpreted) and not based on some ultimate "out there." And the deciders are the rabbis. Would Augustine take the same stance in this situation? Of course not, and for several reasons. First, Augustine would maintain that God speaks to his children all the time, *directly* through scripture. Even more importantly, scripture (and its correct interpretation) could never disagree with God. Yet this is what occurs in the passage above. And God's response could not be more telling. We are told that, after listening to the argument, God laughs and says, "My sons have defeated Me, My sons have defeated Me."

Rabbinic concepts of text and instruction are quite different from Augustine's. Whereas Augustine would maintain a particular, historical truth and then support the application of rhetoric for the transmission of this truth, the rabbis would (and do) argue that the rhetoric (in its broader, educational sense) is all that's important, that the teaching is the text insofar as it allows shifting and polysemy, the production of new texts and, in some sense, a proliferation of history. The metaphysical god of Aristotle and the historical God of Augustine are replaced with what is, for lack of a better term, rhetoric as mitzvah. Rabbinic hermeneutics would thus privilege contingency, practicality, the *now*-ness of knowledge production over an eternal or existential referent (a Passion) of which profession is a (re)performance. In addition, what the example above accomplishes is a denial of direct divine engagement or inspiration, since

> [t]he mode of authority constituted by the House of Midrash is apostolic and institutional; the authority was constituted by Moses at Sinai—it is called Oral Torah—and passed down through a series of institutional relays until it has reached the rabbinic institution, which alone has the authority to decide by its will (that is, by the will of the majority) what is correct for practice. Rabbi Eli'ezer, accordingly, by seeking divine authority for his position was totally undermining the foundations of the entire rabbinic ideology. He was, in effect, denying that the Oral Torah was from Sinai, and it is thus that he puts himself beyond the pale. (Boyarin 169)

God does not engage directly with the world, at least anymore. So, where for John the Logos Ensarkos replaces Torah as the ultimate referent, for the rabbis, Torah (now doubled) supersedes any Logos (139).

Put another way, the rabbis avoid the difficulty Augustine (and Aristotle) runs into regarding the necessary mover and his incarnation by in a sense limiting the arena of possibility (motivation toward action) to two references. In one sense, the Oral can be said to come from the Written, as it is based on the written and is the latter's exposition. But on the other hand, the Oral is essential in order to read the Written text, and in this way can be understood as functioning (formally) prior to written scripture (in much the same way that contemporary theories of reading might place theory before practice). And, in contrast to Aristotle and Augustine, God is left laughing outside of the whole arrangement.

This tradition of study of course remains essential to Jewish thought and practice. For instance, while a prolonged discussion of cross-fertilization between the Greco-Christian and the rabbinic would be beyond the present inquiry, one cannot deny that there is something very Greek about later Jewish exegetical work. But even much later, say, in the 13th century, some important aspects of the practices we are beginning to elucidate here remain.

Often, the practice of midrash is characterized by its apparent contradictions. While an appeal to a particular verse (or part of one) is made, the subsequent commentaries fly off to other verses, other considerations and, depending on which sages are cited and the order of the redaction, it may read like a transcript of arguments among people separated by many years. In one sense, the (probably) much later *Zohar* seems to work the same ground, in as much as it is concerned with wider expectations than those of a particular, single narrative. That is, like midrash, the Zohar is not interested in simply telling a story. In another way, however, the *Zohar* is unlike midrash as it maintains an apparent structure and seems to both offer the promise of an internal integrity to the text under examination and to perform this pulling together itself.

The Tol'Doth section of the *Zohar* begins not with a direct reference to the verse at hand ("These are the generations of Isaac ..."), but with R. Hiya's commentary on "Who can express the mighty acts of the Lord, or make his praises heard? (Ps. cvi, 2)" (*Zohar* Tol'Doth 134a). His response is long. First, R. Hiya addresses those acts by saying "When God resolved to create the world, He used Torah as the plan both of the whole and the parts" (134a). The mighty acts of God can apparently be glossed as the creation of the world, since all subsequent acts by God would relate directly to the first creation. And the Torah is the tool by which God performed this act of acts. This is in keeping with the midrash on Genesis 1, where "The Torah declares, 'I was the working tool of the Holy One, blessed be He'" (*Midrash Rabbah: Genesis* Bereshith I.1). Indeed, R. Hiya says that God tells the world that it is founded "only upon Torah, and therefore I have created man in thee that he may apply himself to its study; otherwise I will turn thee into chaos again" (*Zohar* 134b).

The world is both a whole and made up of parts. Why should it be necessary to mention both, since wholes are usually imagined to be a collection of their parts? In order to make the following relation: "whoever labours in the Torah upholds the world, and enables each part to perform its function" (134b). That is, we may only call the world a whole insofar as each part does what it is supposed to do. Otherwise, the thing falls apart, the center cannot hold, etc.

The *Zohar* thus introduces its focus fairly generally. This is the big picture. God created the world; he used the Torah and the world is founded on Torah; human beings are part of the world whose job it is to study Torah, which is the same thing as studying and upholding the world. We might recognize in this hierarchy something vaguely Greek, inasmuch as it is a hierarchy: first there is God and Torah, then the world as a whole and parts, and finally there are the human beings who have a function in the whole. This seems familiar (see, for instance, Plato's discussion of forms and things in the *Phaedrus*). The *Zohar*'s innovation is to immediately reverse the system and give this new organization equal weight. Here, R. Hiya begins with people:

> For there is not a member in the human body but has its counterpart in the world as a whole. For as man's body consists of members and parts of various ranks all acting and reacting upon each other so as to form one organism, so does the world at large consist of a hierarchy of created things, which when they properly act and react upon each other together form literally one organic body. Thus the whole is organized on the scheme of the Torah, which also consists of sections and divisions which fit into one another and, when properly arranged together, form one organic body. (*Zohar Tol'Doth* 134b)

Where before we began from the most general principle (God's acts) down to the human, here we begin with the human as being equal to (at least in principle) the world which is also (as far as organization is concerned) Torah. This is not simply a bottom-up rereading, but a careful equivalency designed to produce a particular understanding. Things (organs, created plants, bible verses) are important. The parts determine the efficacy of the whole and *are* the whole, as even parts have parts. This is to say that the particular loses none of its particularity when related to the whole organism (body or world), but that very particularity is what determines the big picture. Thus, no hair, no duck, no syllable is unimportant. We should also notice that in both schemes the mediating principle is Torah. This is what allows R. Hiya to say that "all essences both of the higher and the lower grades, of this world and the world to come are to be found [in Torah] " (134b).

Thus, even centuries later, when Jewish exegetes are arguably at their most philosophical, that focus on particulars, on the special and contemporary makeup of the text-as-the-world, remains constant. If the world is continually supported through careful study, then history itself is constantly recreated *now*, and the past is always with us.

Returning to the more distant past, where John and Augustine can be seen as supporting what we have called God in history (Christ as Logos as Love, the Beginning of the greatest story ever told), we might read the Torah of the early rabbis as elaborating *text as history*. That is, scripture is God's covenant, his tool for establishing the world and the people and *history as such*. In such a scheme, Torah might be discussed in terms of immanence inasmuch as "[g]aps are not filled with philosophical ideas but with allusions to or citations of other texts" which are also open to allusions and citations (Boyarin 95). That is, one does not need some extrinsic referent cause—an ideal, a Mover, an uncastrated Father, whatever—from which to depend the truth to which the text can merely refer, but rather the text itself is sufficient to explain itself and the text contains its own principle of genesis. If, as rabbinic practice indicates, the Torah is both the basis of "reality" and, as a discrete book of sentences and paragraphs, may be read as an intertext, as happening in some sense all at the same time, then the two Torahs are both the language of history and history's documentation, its evidence. What, then, is the *act* of Torah?

III. Performance

Piska 161 of *Sifre Deuteronomy* argues from the verse "That he may learn to fear the Lord his God" (17.19): "Hence we learn that fear leads to Scripture, Scripture leads to Targum, Targum leads to Mishna, Mishna leads to Talmud, Talmud leads to performance, performance leads to reverence" (*Sifre: A Tannaitic Commentary on the Book of Deuteronomy* 194). There is text and more text and more text and, finally, performance, which gives way to reverence (thus, through texts fear is translated into reverence). This reverence may be another way of describing the personal investment in the teachings, a belief in the system with the admission that this *belief* is not so much blind faith as it is performance, action, motivation caused by and in response to the text it in turn supports. And logically, reverence gives scripture its significance.

Performance and reverence are the last of the series, but they are also the conditions on which scripture and the texts that emanate from it depend for their power, for their importance. And with every performance there is usually a performer. In a practical sense, especially for halakic matters, the performer is the member of the group. Keeping kosher, for instance, means *participating in* as much as it means *belonging to* a community. Žižek's oppositional formulation is even stronger:

> Christianity involves the distinction between external rules and inner belief (so the question is always: do you REALLY, in the innermost of your heart, believe, or are you just following the dead letter of the law?), while in Judaism, the 'external' rules and practices DIRECTLY ARE the religious belief in its material existence—Jews do not have to DECLARE their belief, they immediately SHOW it in their practice. (*Belief* 128-29)

The focus then is on action, on performance, on adherence to a symbolic system regardless or even in spite of what is in one's "innermost heart."

The difference between these two modes might then be the one outlined by Žižek between faith and belief, worth quoting in full:

> Apropos of the ancient Jews, they BELIEVED IN many gods and spirits, but what Jehovah demanded from them was to HAVE FAITH only in Him, to respect the symbolic pact between the Jewish people and their God who had chosen them [i.e. the covenant with Abraham, Levitican strictures, etc.] One can believe in ghosts without having faith in them, i.e. without believing them (considering them tricky or evil, not feeling bound to them by any pact or commitment); and, in a more tricky but crucial opposite case, one can *believe (have faith in)* X without *believing in X*. The later, for Lacan,[39] is the very case of the big Other, the symbolic Order: "there is no

> big Other," it is just a virtual order, a shared fiction, we do not have to believe IN IT in order to believe IT, to feel bound by some symbolic commitment. For that very reason, in the case of the imaginary "belief in," belief is always displaced (it is never me who, in the first person singular, is ready to assume belief, there is always the need for the fiction of a "subject supposed to belief" [sic.]), while in the case of symbolic faith, the commitment to the first person singular is performatively assumed. (109-110)

It is this weird final possibility that seems most like what rabbinic Judaism introduces. By that I do not mean to say that rabbis or other Jewish people do not believe in God. The point is that belief in God is not a necessary precondition for being Jewish, but faith (as adherence to the symbolic pact) is. Under these terms, one can conceive of being both atheist and Jewish, but probably not atheist and Christian. In rabbinic Judaism, performance is what counts, and precision in acting is something that can be transmitted, taught.

In terms of interpretation and education, the performer of Scripture-Targum-Mishna-Talmud is primarily the teacher, the sage, and then secondarily the student who learns by example. And this performance is also Torah. Martin Jaffee describes the rabbis after the Second Temple as supreme examples of such Torah:

> Among such teachers, the name *Torah* did not simply refer to the books they interpreted or to the substance of their teaching; more important, they seemed to exude Torah from their very persons, so that it took form in the contours of a human life. In such men, a principle of being had become tangible to the senses for interpretation and emulation. (86)

Indeed, Jaffee argues that the substance of oral Torah was in fact the rabbis themselves and that written versions carried much less weight than the physical presence of the sage in the midst of sagifying. We should note here that there is something almost classical (read Geek) in this stress on performance.[40] Of course, this stress on the virtuosity of the sage translates to students, too. There is a midrash:

> Rab Judah said in the name of Rab:
>
> > When Moses ascended on high he found the Holy One, blessed be He, engaged in affixing coronets to the letters. Said

Moses, "Lord of the Universe, Who stays Thy hand?" He answered, "There will arise a man, at the end of many generations, Akiba b. Joseph by name, who will expound upon each tittle heaps and heaps of laws." "Lord of the Universe," said Moses; "permit me to see him." He replied, "Turn thee round". Moses went and sat down behind eight rows [and listened to the discourses upon the law]. Not being able to follow their arguments he was ill at ease, but when they came to a certain subject and the disciples said to the master "Whence do you know it?" and the latter replied "It is a law given unto Moses at Sinai" he was comforted. (*Midrash Rabbah: Genesis* B. Menahot 29b)

There are few points made by this short passage. First is the principle of close reading, so that even the decorative bits of the letters carry meaning. Next is the matter of the sage expounding knowledge of the text via performance, as we have already described. What follows is peculiar, since Moses himself (who ostensibly received both Torahs at Sinai) is sitting at the back of the class, as a beginning student. The idea is that a student gradually moves up, row by row, until he is eventually standing at the front of the class, a teacher himself. The image is as striking as it is paradoxical. Moses is the "father" of the faith who is in essence superseded by the rabbis. And although he is unable to follow the arguments, he is comforted by the attribution to "Moses at Sinai." We should likely be reminded of the rabbinic response mentioned before—"It is not in heaven"—as this midrash also established the importance of rabbinic interpretation over the text's origin. Important, too, is an implied theme of the sage as a kind of perfected student, since Akiba is essentially a student of Moses, if several times removed.

As an example of the student assuming the teacher's position, there is Hillel:

For they said of Hillel the Elder that each day he would labor and earn a half-dinar. Half of it he would give to the registrar of the collegium, and half went to support himself and his dependents. One time he was unable to earn anything, and the registrar of the collegium denied him entry. So he climbed up and sat against the opening of the skylight in order to hear the words of the Living God from the mouths of Shemaiah and Avtalion.

Now that day was a Sabbath Eve in the dead of winter, and snow fell upon him from Heaven. When the Morning Start rose, said Shemaiah to Avtalion: Avtalion, my brother, on most days the house is bright, but today it is dark—is it cloudy out? They glanced and saw the shape of a man in the skylight. They climbed up and found him covered in three cubits of snow. They brought him down, bathed him, anointed him, and sat him next to the fireplace. They said: This Hillel—for him it's worth desecrating the Sabbath! (B. Yoma 35b, quoted in Jaffee 91-92)

First, since I work at a university with a number of commuter students, the fact of Hillel's splitting his wages seems absolutely common to contemporary situations, though the fact of his almost freezing to death is not very common.[41] Regardless, the lesson of the story comes from the recognition that we are not given the Torah uttered by the teachers in the collegium. We have no idea of even what they were speaking about. Instead, we are given Hillel's frozen but listening form and the sages' agreement that "for him it's worth desecrating the Sabbath." Jaffee explains, "More important than the oral Torah Hillel failed to hear is the oral Torah he became by his desire to learn" (92). Hillel eventually becomes one of the greatest sages and even teaches at the same school, but he becomes a teacher, it seems, at the very moment of his perfection as a student.

IV. In Other Terms

Performance, and not some extrinsic cause or exception, is therefore what is essential to rabbinic Judaism. And performance as the means by which the people is maintained is a response to God's absence *now*. In contrast, the Christian economy depends on the injection of God into history as the Logos to which everything else (in its insufficiency) refers. If I were bold enough to translate these two economies into psychoanalytic terms, I might look to Lacanian sexuation[42] and write the Christian situation with:

$\exists x \overline{\Phi x}$, marking the father-function which effectively allows for the delimiting of the set of all men by positing the excep-

> tion or necessarily excluded term—there is one (the Mover, God, or here the uncastrated Father) who does not fall under the phallic function, and

> $\forall x \Phi x$, indicating that therefore all men fall under the phallic function or, as Lacan puts it, "it is through the phallic function that man as whole acquires his inscription." (*Encore* 79)

This phallic function is precisely castration as the mark or cut that is the lack or negativity around which the subject coalesces and it is what allows for the collection of all these (masculine) subjects under one heading, thereby allowing for the signifier *man*. That heading may be "man," but I guess it could also be "Church" or something else. And, since this is a *masculine* economy, perhaps it might have something to say about the Church's much-touted historic sexism? At least it does seem to indicate why the appellation "father" might be so important.

Keeping with Lacan's formulation, the rabbinic Jewish side of things would be written as the feminine:

> $\overline{\exists x \Phi x}$, where there is not one exception to the rule (there is not one who does not fall under the phallic function) so that the set remains unconstrained, and

> $\overline{\forall x} \Phi x$, so that the subject thus inscribed "will not allow for any universality—it will be not-whole, insofar as it has the choice of positing itself in Φx [phallic function] or of not being there." (*Encore* 80)

The final indeterminacy of the subject in relation to the phallic function is most useful if we consider that perhaps what is illustrated by the first line on the feminine side of the diagram is not a logical and necessary Mover, Cause, or God but something else that is by its nature unbounded, not-whole or always already incomplete; insofar as there is no necessary closure for the set, there is no completed set. This seems to describe the Torah as we have elaborated it so far and, at the very least, my psychoanalytic chutzpah here has allowed another way of describing the immanence of Torah and the rhetorical nature (the timeliness) of its performance, since one way of rendering the subject's relation to the Other from the feminine position is via some demand from the Other which provokes the subject to respond with the question "Am I a man or a woman?" That is, am I wholly within the phallic function or not wholly in it?

Certainly, the invocation of sexuation is problematic here in that it raises all sorts of questions about possible relationship between (patristic) Christianity and (rabbinic) Judaism. Is the term "Judeo-Christian" the equivalent of a contemporary married woman's hyphenated last name? Well, yes, at least from the Christian perspective. In the sense that the hyphenate suggests a move from one to the other, even tells the story of an exchange, it is certainly in keeping with the (Christian) myth that Christianity completes Judaism (thus eliding it). But as we have seen, Daniel Boyarin claims that Christianity and rabbinic Judaism become systems (and "religions") at roughly the same time and in contradistinction (this is the argument of his book *Border Lines*). So, if Boyarin is correct (and maybe even if he is not), then Judaism as we have described it is not the precursor to Christianity but its contemporary.

This broaches perhaps my biggest difficulty with Žižek's recent work on Christianity. In both *On Belief* and *The Puppet and the Dwarf*, Žižek assumes that Christianity somehow grows from Judaism, though in various and interesting ways. Using Paul as his transition figure is useful, then, as Paul is the Jew who opens membership up to gentiles. The point to be made is that Paul is not the same kind of Jew as those rabbis who wrote down and codified Oral Torah. Paul is not responding to those rabbis when he is speaking of Law, but rather to some degree the rabbis are responding to him. Additionally, Žižek's God is not nearly as nuanced as the God we described for Augustine in the previous chapter, and it seems to me that one cannot simply assume the *identical-ness* of the Father and Son (and so present God as the Lacanian split subject) without also addressing the father-son dynamic in some way and acknowledging the two- and even three-ness of God in ecclesiastical understanding as the two-powers-in-heaven position takes the lead in Christianity. In essence, what I object to is Žižek's easy Christianizing of Lacanian psychoanalysis by way of ignoring certain aspects of both Christianity and Judaism. On the other hand, Žižek's insistence on an "authentic" Pauline Christianity does serve a revolutionary purpose, as it functions as a kind of protest against Protestants insofar as his return is in clear opposition to contemporary versions of the faith. So a kinder reading of Žižek's work would be as perhaps an informed misreading that is really addressing contemporary concerns. Žižek's work thus is neither solely philosophy nor critical theory, but is primarily rhetorical.[43]

Of course, by invoking Lacanian notions of sexuation as a way of describing two different relations to an Other, I have also gendered rabbinic Judaism feminine, which may or may not be a problem.[44] If I am serious about the metaphor, do I need to modify the famous Lacanian aphorism and seriously develop upon the statement "La juif n'exist pas"? Probably not, since the place the Jew has held historically in the Christian imagination[45] should be obvious and this Semite is never an actual Jewish person. In fact, anti-Semitism points to the split subject of the masculine side of sexuation (the side on which I've placed the Christian) insofar as, as Žižek makes clear,

> the standard theory of "projection," according to which the anti-Semite "projects" on to the figure of the Jew the disavowed part of himself, is not sufficient: the figure of the "conceptual Jew" cannot be reduced to the externalization of my (anti-Semite's) "inner conflict"; on the contrary, it bears witness to (and tries to cope with) the fact that I am originally decentred, part of an opaque network whose meaning and logic elude my control. (*Plague* 9)

What Žižek elaborates is that, from the masculine side, fantasy is a way to deal with some radical anxiety by giving body to a lack and then placing it outside. Historically, women have served this function. And so have Jews. What may need some more detail, however, is what this gendering means in terms of what I am claiming about the rabbinic relationship with God, this latter being the ostensible Other of any discussion about religion.

The previous chapter (in other terms) discussed the binitarian nature of God as necessary in order for there to be a divine physical presence of consequence and that the correspondence of the two is Love (as Logos Ensarkos and as the Third Person—a remainder—after the Passion). The result of this economy is, according to Žižek's account, a debt owed to God for his Love qua mercy (*Belief* 145). In essence, the driving activity of all Christians is to live up to the event of the Passion, to respond appropriately to God's Love by being Christ-like, by loving him (and the Father) back. As Lacan says it, "[t]o put it plainly, by loving God, we love ourselves, and by first loving ourselves—'well-ordered charity', as it is put—we pay the appropriate homage to God" (*Encore* 70-71).

The obverse of this, then, would to be the beloved of God, and this is the situation in which the rabbinic Jews find themselves. Except, as we have seen, it isn't really God with whom they seem to have a relationship, but Torah. In God's absence, the text in *its* binitarian nature functions as an Other (that is barred, bifurcated into Oral and Written) to which every question is addressed and by which the world itself is sustained. That is, first there may have been God's direct involvement, but now there is Torah: On Psalms 136, R. Joshua b. Levi said: "To what do these twenty-six [verses of] 'Give thanks' [Psalms 136] correspond? To the twenty-six generations which the Holy One, blessed be He, created in His world; though He did not give them the Torah, He sustained them by His love" (*Soncino Talmud*. Pesachim 118a). The implication is that Torah supersedes love *now* and what the two Torahs indicate is a demand to engage with Torah, to perform and even be it, in order to maintain a people that in some way stand for the physical presence of the divine in his absence. Where the first chapter describes a necessary separation from the divine that demands love to work, here is a contingent practice that sustains the subject both of and as enunciation.

3 But the Greatest of These Is Love

> *. . . in the sublime, as in great fortunes, there must be something which is overlooked.*
>
> —Longinus

Over twenty years ago, friends of mine had entries in an annual student film festival. Most of the films were low-budget affairs, depending on one or two gimmicks to rise above financial and technical limitations. Many were ingenious. But one short film was longer than the rest, nearly fifteen minutes, and had a giant budget in comparison with the others. Shot on expensive 35 mm color film stock, it told the story of a soldier caught behind enemy lines who, alone with his rifle, had to fight his way back home. Already, this is a pretty familiar setup. As the soldier burst through brush, leaped over stumps, climbed low hills, all the while dodging bullets from enemy soldiers apparently staggered across the route especially to get him, the audience began to shift in the seats, grumble, and eventually several voices were actually yelling at the screen "Shoot him!". Finally, after so much danger, the hero saw the line of trenches marking home and safety. Predictably, just yards from the base, a single shot mortally wounded the soldier and he fell to the ground. Cheering came from the crowd, followed by a universal groan and shouts of "No!" as the dying soldier reached toward his left breast pocket.

The hero pulled out a photograph of a girl. And, of course, the crowd could not tolerate this last cliché. It is possible that, given the context of a feature-length study instead of a scene, this final gesture to a gal back home might have warranted a less hostile reaction, though the moment would not have been less cliché. At least there is the opportunity to hide cliché behind new, distracting drapes. But extracted, amplified as it was, the film foregrounded a particular false resolution that, at one time at least, must have been quite adequate. The lone soldier trapped behind enemy lines, presumably on some mission to secure the safety of his country against foreign aggressors, in the end is sacrificed for that country. And the picture of his love (the girl is an index for homeland here) has the effect of making the military and political tangle very personal. He has died for his love, has sacrificed his life to protect her chaste image. Beautiful, unless we also imagine that the whack-a-mole enemy soldiers also likely had photos of their true loves and were just as likely to die for them.

Love has often been linked to sacrifice, in particular self-sacrifice, and to violence. Elsewhere I have discussed love in terms of how one may approach literary texts.[46] While we might agree that, at least in the popular conception, there are many *kinds* of love—for a pet, for one's children, for Joyce—we really do use the same word to describe them all and have been writing about our love for whatever for a very long time.

I. What Is Sacrifice?

In *Things Hidden since the Foundation of the World*, René Girard claims that the founding mechanism for religion and, indeed, culture as such, is mimetic rivalry. That is, Girard finds evidence of conflict between rivals over an object that quickly becomes irrelevant in the fight as each claimant takes on the features of the other and soon loses any discrete identity. In essence, each side of contention presumes the other's bad faith, or rather, presumes that the other party is the cause of the conflict. As a result, motives tend toward those of revenge and not acquisition, per se. "In such cases," says Girard, "in its perfection and paroxysm mimesis becomes a chain reaction of vengeance, in which human beings are constrained to the monotonous repetition of homicide. Vengeance turns them into doubles" (12). Breaking this pattern is, according to Girard, the innovation of Christ who, far from adopting the usual mode of reconciliation—the displaced, despised sacrifice or scapegoat—clearly moves against this mechanism in hopes of both revealing its workings and denying its effect.

While it is difficult to ignore the larger ramifications of Girard's theory of the founding mechanism and mimetic rivalry in their apparent universality and many variations, the job here will be to consider closely his explication of text, what he calls the Judgment of Solomon

(I Kings 3.16-28) as markedly anti-sacrificial and as a type or figure for the Christic innovation.

In this narrative, two "harlots" come before King Solomon, each claiming that the living son is theirs. Girard is quick to point out that in the story, at least at the beginning, both women are treated identically; "that both of the women are described as 'harlots' underlines the lack of differentiation between them" (238). One might add here that, as harlots, there is apparently no paternal claim on the child. Indeed, one might extend speculation and suggest that in place of paternal authority is Solomon himself as the one who decides the dispute, as the function of the Law proper. Regardless, each of the women makes her claim and, in lieu of any way of discriminating, Solomon calls for a sword in order to cut the child in half, thereby giving each claimant (at least a portion of) the contested object.

The child is, after all, and especially at these initial stages, an *object* of contention. That is, the child is the object of desire for both parties inasmuch as he is what would decide one woman's position as mother over the other. In addition, the rivalry is not simply over who "owns" the living object, but also who owns the dead one. Essentially, while the two women are both making claims of motherhood for the living boy, there is an implicit blame placed against the other as murderer (or at least killer). The situation is, then, one concerned as much with blame as with ownership, and it is not a far leap to include this notion of blame in Girard's claims about vengeance. Each mother is effectively saying, "She killed her own son and has now stolen mine."

Solomon's call for the sword provokes two responses. The text has the first mother (which it immediately differentiates from the other by calling her "the woman whose son was alive") give up her claim on the boy in order to save him. The other woman says "It shall be neither mine nor yours; divide it" (Girard 237). The narrative difficulty here is obvious. The sense seems to be that the first mother cedes her son *and then* the second mother calls for his death, which does not make much narrative sense, since the second mother would more likely simply accept the son; she has won, after all. One might read the two responses as concurrent in order to reconcile this difficulty, though the text does not say that they were. However, Solomon's response is well known. The child is given to the first woman because it is somehow clear that she is the real mother.

Of the first ruling of Solomon, Girard suggests that "[t]here is an element of logic and justice in this royal decision. But the justice, which is purely formal, conceals a terrible injustice, since the child is not an object that can be divided in two. To do so would kill the child. By this murder the true mother will be deprived of her living child" (238).

What Girard seems to suggest (but does not take up meaningfully) is that, at a certain point, the child is exactly such an object in that it is *only* an object of desire disputed by two claimants, two rivals, who want it. In this light, Solomon's move to divide the child should be read as wholly ethical in that it seeks to reconcile the rivalry by removing the object of desire. Girard, of course, gives Solomon's wisdom more credit and assumes that the decision is a ploy. The point to be made here is that the child is only "the living child" when compared to the dead one. The child is an object to be desired in one sense only because there is another child that is not desired. Solomon offers to level the field by simply making both children dead and so killing desire proper.

This option is exactly what the second mother calls for. Killing the child—and in effect killing the desire supporting it as an object—is the only way to maintain a particular distance toward the other mother; neither will have a son, but both will be maintained in the economy of rivalry in the absence of the object, or in its death. One could imagine the debate continuing over which dead child belongs to which mother, over who killed her son and whose son was killed, etc.

But the child is not killed. Instead, the "good" mother cedes her claim to the child so that the child may live. And what is such a ceding if not the ceding of desire as such, of giving up her desire for the sake of its object? Girard argues that one should not read this ceding by the real mother in sacrificial terms, even though she "cannot be sure that her sudden decision to renounce the child will not be interpreted *unfavorably to her*. . . . She has no means of anticipating the monarch's 'divine wisdom'. So she risks her own life" (240). Girard says that what is of secondary importance to the real mother—her renunciation and her personal risk— is foregrounded by the language of sacrifice. He suggests that her true and primary concern is nothing but the safety of the child that was, at least at the beginning, the object of desire for both rivals.

As much as one can determine the motives of this woman, we should probably go along with this reading. Certainly, it seems to be the interpretation supporting the wisdom of Solomon. But one might also suggest that what Girard misses is that what is primary to the real mother is that the child should live *even if it should live without her*. This is not a simple combination of the primary and secondary motives that Girard presents, but is an innovation itself. The "without her" above makes no reference to the state of the mother, per se, but rather to the state of the child in terms of having a (real) mother at all. That is, by ceding her claim on the child (as the object of contention), the good mother assumes its place as a missing cause, as what must be excluded from the rivalry in order to end it definitively and for the child to survive in this new economy. That is, the rivalry itself is barred or negated by the real mother via a lie. For the child to remain whole (and living, no longer just an object), the real mother must remove herself, assume the position of the lost cause of the rivalry, the position of desire as such, and therefore become the absent foundation on (or because of) which the child becomes more than an object of contention and so can take up a new place in terms of the Law. By ceding her desire, the real mother (kind of) gets it, too. What she offers is not her life, but her motherhood, her place in the system. The child would live and take its place in the system by virtue of this cutting, shearing, a loss that marks the real mother's desire. It is only her response that allows Solomon's wisdom to shine.

Apparently, this ceding is not a sacrifice. Girard links sacrifice with the "ultimately positive nature of violence," and we are dealing here with a substantive absence (195). What this means is that, when the real mother gives up her desire, she does it for the sake of its object (who then becomes something other than an object) and she assumes the role of what must be excluded from the economy in order for any deal to work. As we will see, this is the position of the mother, and for Julia Kristeva, as one who assumes abjection so that the child may find (and found) a place with/in Law and is precisely the mark of love. Such a position is exactly the exception that propagates Law.

How, then, might the above economy relate to Christ and the Passion? Girard seems to place Christ on the side of the good mother. And such a rough equation seems to work when he states that "all of Christ's words and deeds . . . are determined by his will to save a humanity unable to see that all the old sacrificial solutions [read here Solomon's first solution] are now bankrupt and completely empty" (241).

The added difficulty is that, while the good mother gets her child, Christ has to die. That is, he must leave the economy completely in order to reemerge as something quite different, as something resurrected. But one might also suggest that the real mother is also transformed, inasmuch as she is no longer simply one harlot among two (or many), but the mother of the living child who, by ceding her desire, gets to keep it as something different, as an object reconfigured in relation to the (for Kristeva, paternal) Law. As we turn next to Julia Kristeva, one might find that Christianity, as set up in Girard's reading of the Gospels, is Judaism plus the abject. Christianity is the law with its exception, and perhaps this is one of the meanings Paul intends when he writes that to be Christ-like is to be in the world but not of it.

In the fourth chapter of her *Powers of Horror*, Julia Kristeva asserts a reading of the biblical pure/impure binary and its relevance to sacrifice. We might mention that such a reading, based as it is on a particular text, is (at least generally) exegetical. That is, her claim is that she is presenting something that is already there, latent in the pages, a code that just needs to be brought out. Of course, the assumption that anything can be *brought out* implies also the act of interpretation insofar as it indicates a choice, since some words or ideas will not be foregrounded because they are not relevant, are confusing, or simply don't fit into the schema. Such is probably necessary and unavoidable when one wants to say anything about a text. The point in mentioning the situation here is that this present discussion is intended to bring out certain issues in Kristeva's text that might complicate the picture she gives of impurity, sacrifice, and the feminine. The goal is not to say that she is fundamentally wrong or that the biblical account does not indicate a patriarchal, phallocratic system. Rather, that this is *not all* it does.

That Kristeva makes such a claim is evident when she writes that "biblical impurity is permeated with defilement; in that sense it points to, but does not signify an autonomous force that can be threatening for divine agency" and this force may be seen in "the cathexis of maternal function—mother, women, reproduction" (90). Certainly, much of biblical regulation is caught up in differentiating pure and impure, clean and unclean, and she argues persuasively for relating these binaries to the feminine. We will work through this last later. First, however, we should consider the binary opposition she claims both in her terms and in the terms of the text she is explicating.

"From its very beginning," writes Kristeva, "the biblical text insists on maintaining the distance between man and God by means of a dietary differentiation" (95). She goes on to point to human expulsion from the garden as the means of establishing a dietary prohibition "in order to forestall the chaos that would result from the identification of man with the immortality of God." This seems absolutely accurate if (and only if) we stress the *maintaining* of this distance, not its establishing. Before the human violation of the first prohibition, the human is already separate from God. In the eighteenth verse of the second chapter of Genesis, immediately following the prohibition against eating from the Tree of Knowledge, God decides that humankind should not be alone.[47] So God sets out to create a partner and produces, from the dust, all of the animals:

> So out of the ground the Lord God formed every animal of the field and every bird of the air, and brought them to [humankind] to see what [it] would call them; and whatever [humankind] called every living creature, that was its name. [Humankind] gave names to all cattle and to the birds of the air, and to every animal of the field; but for [humankind] there was not found a helper as [its] partner. (Genesis 2.19-20)

According to this creation narrative, God is creating companions for the first human and is making these companions in the same way he created the first human; the goal of these creations is to produce "a helper" and "partner" for the first human being. So one might read these creations as an attempt on God's part to reproduce the original trick of creating humanity, and humankind gives names to the animals that were apparently intended to be its equal. Not only is the human obviously different from the animals, but we are shown a new development in its attributes: speech and naming. Here we should stress two points. First, God is for some reason unable to reproduce his original trick. He cannot seem to make a new person, a helper. Secondly, we are made aware of this fact through the human act of speaking, of naming. In effect, we might read the human naming of the animals as a metonymy of no's: "that's not me, it's a robin; and that's not me, it's a tuna...." Finally, God must take another human from the first one, by cutting it away from its identical self. Only then can humankind say, "this is at last bone of my bone, flesh of my flesh" (Genesis 2.23a).

What we find, then, is a difference, a distance, between God and the human established before the violation of any prohibition. What makes the dietary so important is not the establishing of distance as such, but the realization of it by the first man and woman. So Kristeva is perhaps imprecise when she states that "food effects an initial division between man and God; to God belong living beings (by way of sacrifice), to man vegetable foods" (96). At least, such is not borne out by this myth; the division is already clear before any eating or sacrifice, though not clear to the two humans. But we might agree with her that the animals do belong to God. Along with the rest of the world. God apparently walked in the cool of the evening and, after the original sin of understanding, God's curses involve the antipathetic relationship between humanity and nature. These may all be read as further signs of separation from the divine, since the world is God's.[48] Of the curses, the first concerns the serpent. It might be worthwhile to note that the result of this curse is to "put enmity between you and the woman, and between your offspring and hers" (Genesis 3.15). While it would be a gigantic leap to make matrilineal claims here, this language does trouble the assumption of an all-pervasive patriarchy. Of the curses God pronounces on the humans, the first are pain in childbirth, woman's subjugation to her husband (okay, some patriarchy here), and the ground's animosity toward man. In both cases, engagement with what might be termed "the natural world" engenders pain, difficulty, and finally, expulsion from the garden where the human and the divine could commune on common ground.[49]

The next concern is the practice of sacrifice. Kristeva claims that sacrifice is determined by what is pure and impure, and here we might not quibble (97). Certainly, some things (and animals) are inappropriate for bringing into the tabernacle or temple.[50] Assuming that these practices ultimately relate to a maternal which is always being effaced (as I understand Kristeva's claim) and that the separation of "inside" and "outside" are called into question by the mother, we might suggest that sacrificial practice does something of the same if we extend the metaphor to encompass inside and outside human culture. Priests must be purified before entering the holy space. That is, they must be wholly separate from the "natural world." But, in cultic practice, after the sacrifice of the burnt offering, the priest was to remove his ritual clothing and take the ashes of the offering to a place outside the camp (Lev. 6.10), where the scapegoat "shall be set free in the wilderness"

(Lev. 6.10, Lev. 6.22). Here, the abjected is moved out of the community, not only from the cleanest place (the temple), but also from the ring of civilization to mediate between it and the dirty wilderness surrounding the people. It is let loose there precisely because such distinctions hold no power outside the community separated from God. Indeed, it all returns to God. And God takes care of the mess.[51]

Kristeva accurately turns to the ultimate mark of the Hebrew covenant with God: circumcision. After indicating the peculiar placing of the maternal question between dietary prohibitions and the sick body in Leviticus (which is fascinating, but outside our purview here), she discusses the different cultic practices a new mother must observe, which depend on whether the child is male or female. If the child is female, the mother must offer a burnt offering and a sin offering in order to purify herself.

From what defilement does she necessarily need purification? Obviously, the birth itself, as Kristeva makes clear. What we might suggest here, however, is that it is possible to read birthing as such as participation in what we are calling "the natural world." That is, giving birth was likened above to the land (which, by extension, is the wilderness surrounding the people) and is a mark of the animal (since this biological act makes apparent our affinity with them), both of which humanity has been separated from, since the world is in a sense divine and the animals belong to God. Our point is that the pervading fear (and abjection) of the biological that Kristeva finds throughout the Hebrew Bible *may* more generally be rendered as insistence on the separation of humanity (or at least the chosen people) from God (who is then aligned with both the clean and the dirty). In these terms, Kristeva is correct in indicating that the maternal blurs the lines between inside and outside, but in our economy this makes the mother abject only when she takes on an aspect of God. She is not wholly of/in the symbolic order. What the insistence on sacrifice effectively does is force her back onto one (admittedly patriarchal) side of the arrangement. It is also what allows (or forces) her to worship.

Of course, if the child is male, something else happens. The male child is circumcised and no sacrifice is given. As Kristeva states:

> Circumcision would thus separate one from maternal, feminine impurity and defilement; it stands instead of sacrifice, meaning that it not only replaces it but is its equivalent—a sign of the alliance with God. Circumcision can be said to

find its place in the same series as food taboos; it indicates a separation and at the same time does away with the need for sacrifice, of which it nevertheless bears the trace. (99)

In light of our previous discussion, we might amend the above. The alliance with God of which Kristeva writes is an alliance through separation.[52] In this way, the separation from "maternal, feminine impurity and defilement" is also a separation from the divine. We may read what follows differently than Kristeva intends:

> I agree that [circumcision] concerns an alliance with the God of the chosen people; but what the male is separated from, the other that circumcision carves out on his very sex, is the other sex, impure, defiled. By repeating the natural scar of the umbilical cord at the location of sex, by duplicating and thus displacing through ritual the preeminent separation, which is that from the mother, Judaism seems to insist in symbolic fashion—the very opposite of what is "natural"—that the identity of the speaking being (with his God) is based on the separation of the son from his mother. Symbolic identity presupposes the violent differences of the sexes. (100)

Part of her point is certainly useful. Circumcision (and prohibition) does function as a replacement for sacrifice. But the alliance with God is one of covenant, something (literally) cut between two parties who are fundamentally separate. So what Kristeva reads as the "preeminent separation, which is from the mother" is always already also a separation from the divine through speech, the efficacy of which is first symbolized by the covenant cut with Abraham. And if circumcision is a "symbolic" mark of the "natural scar" of the umbilical cord, it is also a permanent, bodily trace of it.

Regardless, to insist from this evidence that the "identity of the speaking being" is predicated on the separation of mother and son simply does not work, at least in these particular texts. Separation existed before there was sex. In fact, the advent of the sexes depended upon the ability of the human to speak, to say *no* to God in the presence of so many animals, which were not human precisely because they could be named as different. And it is because of this radical separation that the first mother is cut from sexless humanity, that sex is established at the moment of its utterance. "She shall be called woman" (Genesis 2.23) *because* she is somehow like/from me.

II. Love Is the Word

In *Sacrificed Lives*, Martha Reineke explains rather concisely the trajectory of her thought and work: "This project makes the work of René Girard central to its theorizing about sacrifice, as Kristeva has not done, drawing on Kristeva as well as on Girard to set forth an expanded theory of sacrifice" (73). Reineke is able to draw both theorists together, highlighting their similarities and their blind spots. Indeed, she so adeptly weaves the two together that the resulting fabric is very fine. Nothing seems to get through. But where Reineke offers whole cloth, our discussion is more concerned with stitches, with seams, and ultimately, with the thread. That is, *this* writing has less to say about the sacrificial mechanisms and their prehistory than about the predicates for theorizing about them. Reineke's language above suggests such an inquiry when agency is given to the project itself—to "its theorizing"—as if texts, even new ones, have minds of their own. Which they apparently do.

For our purposes, then, we should accept everything Girard has to say about the founding mimeticism (the model and rivalry) as the conditions for culture, per se, and as the mechanism by which culture, at least to a point, reiterates itself. And Kristeva's positing of the abject as that which marks or remains of pre-objectal relations supports the above assumption if we acknowledge the scapegoat as another word for the abject. What is less obvious, perhaps, and what may take some digging, is how the two theorists' responses to the obscene condition of the individual and culture offer an answer with similar predications. Indeed, as we look at the nature of the text—Christ, love, and abjection in their works—we may discover that the two thinkers are similar not only in what they offer to the theoretical conversation (as Reineke shows), but in that they spring from a common source.

René Girard's relation of/to the Gospels does not seem all that peculiar at first reading. That he assigns an agency to them is obvious. After all, according to Girard, the Gospels offer the singular answer to mimetic violence as it proliferates in and is repeated by culture. Still, one often reports that a text *teaches* something, the text *shows* its readers, or simply that the text *says* ____. What we usually mean is, given that any text is an attempt at communication, the text *seems to say* what we are reading from it. That is, there is an understood author who is speaking through the text. This is at least the vulgar notion. More sophisticated thinkers and readers would of course acknowledge that what one seems to hear from a text is not all made up of some author's intentions. Readers bring things to the text, too, if only vocabulary, cultural tendencies, even motives. In these terms, what a text can (seem to) say is determined by a matrix of relationships and is overdetermined from the cultural sphere down to the individual. There is thus a sense in which the text itself does speak, since what it says is not so much determined by authorial intent or even the use to which it is put by its readers as it is by the interrelation of both of these with the larger culture and the time of day and what music is playing in the coffee shop. In this understanding, texts *are* independent, at least as much as anything (or anybody) can be. And such a notion allows the text to say new things all the time, which is nice for literature programs.

Of course, there is probably a difference between any old book and texts that can be called holy. Religious texts are words from God, and while it is possible for readers to misinterpret or to misread, it is unlikely that God could be constrained by the vagaries of reading in the same way mortal authors are. Augustine says as much in *On Christian Teaching*. Girard says as much, too, but in a manner more complicated than even Augustine would likely follow. In discussing the non-sacrificial nature of the Passion, Girard writes that his reading "is rooted in the Gospels themselves, in their own subversion of sacrifice, which restores the original text" (181). We shall return to "the original text" soon, but here we should notice that Girard conceives of a text that not only says or teaches, but a writing that *does* something in the world. The Gospels subvert and, in an even bolder move, the Gospels "deprive God of his most essential role in primitive religions—that of polarizing everything mankind does not succeed in mastering, particularly in relationships between individuals" (183). A very active text indeed. The point here is that, while the issue is ostensibly Girard's reading of the text (a reading apparently few have made since the writing of the Gospels), what is called for is rather a *hearing* of the text, since this message is what the Gospels have always already been saying. That people have not before been able to hear what the Gospels are saying is testimony to the power of mimetic conflict. That the Gospels still keep saying what they do is evidence of God's love.

The Gospels speak of the Passion of Christ, and this is what may be meant by *the original text*. Girard argues that "[b]y rejecting the sacrificial reading of the Passion, we arrive at a simpler, more direct and more coherent reading, enabling us to integrate all the gospel themes into a seamless totality" (182). That any notion of a seamless totality would be problematic for students of literature, say, or even history, should not bother us, since the text is made of God's words, not ours. Rather, the above gives us a glimpse of the trajectory of Girard's understanding of the nature of this text as it relates to God, an understanding he will certainly make more explicit. The Passion is the truth of scripture. It is, indeed, its subject, and we must read the restoration of *the original text* as the non-sacrificial reading of *the Passion*. They are one and the same, and this revelation is the Christian twist on the sublime image illustrated by Longinus.

We can be more reductive. It is Christ himself (through the Passion he instantiates) that is the text, since Jesus is God's Word. Girard argues: "To say that Jesus dies, not as a sacrifice, but in order that there may be no more sacrifices, is to recognize in him the Word of God.... Rather than become a slave of violence, as our own word necessarily does, the Word of God says no to violence" (210). Jesus is the physical manifestation of this Word, he is its literalization, and here we should note that the Word is recognized outright as a force different from our own words. It takes on the characteristic of a proper name. As such, it is not a text to be interpreted, but rather a gospel—a new discourse—to be heard, if only we can manage it.

We might inquire more directly as to the nature of this Word. What does it mean to say "no to violence"? Even more generally, what does it mean to literalize a word? Girard argues:

> ... the gospel text contains an explicit revelation of the foundations of all religions in victimage, and this revelation takes place thanks to a non-violent deity—the Father of Jesus—for this revelation appears in close association between Father and Son, in their common nature, and in the idea, repeated several times in John, that Jesus is the only way to the Father, that he is himself the same thing as the Father, that he is not only the Way, but the Truth and the Life. Indeed, this is why those who have seen Jesus have seen the Father himself. (184)

The revelation above is "the knowledge of violence and all its works" (208). We discussed this "close association between Father and Son" in the first chapter and called it Love. For Girard, the Son-Father relationship is, in essence, non-violence by means of revealing the victimage mechanism. If this is the Word as Jesus—which is at the same time the Word of God—and this word is in one sense a strict "no to violence," then in what manner does it offer an alternative to mimetic violence? That is, given that God says no, to what does he say yes?

Girard's reasoning is direct on this point. At the beginning of his discussion of the difference between the Greek and Johannine Logos, Girard first simply allows that logos "is a term which designates Christ as redeemer, in so far as he is closely identified with the creative work of God and with God himself" (263). This seems to work with the above longer quotation, as Jesus-as-Word appears in the "association between" Father and Son or is simply "identified" with it. We should notice, however, that two slightly different formulations are being offered. In the first, the truth of non-violence is to be found in the relation between Father and Son, "in their common nature." In the second version, Christ as redeemer (and as the Word, one supposes) is located between God himself and his creative work. The difference depends on how one reads this creative work. In the economy Girard has been positing, it seems likely that we should read this work as nothing but Jesus the Son. Of course, this would not be creative but generative work, since the idea is that Jesus came from God, is the Son of the Father, and is God. Regardless, what is suggested is that there are, if not two Words existing simultaneously, then two meanings of the Word in which we might find both the no and the yes.

Girard's answer to this second meaning of the Word is elegant. He states:

> If the Father is as the Son describes him, the Word of the Son…is indeed the Word of the Father. It is not gratuitous representation; it describes the very being of the Father. It invites us to become like the Father, by behaving as he behaves. The Word of the Father, which is identical with the Father, consists in telling mankind what the Father is, so that people will be able to imitate him: "Love your enemies, pray for your persecutors, so shall you be sons of your Father." (269)

Word is Word is Word. And the Word consists both in telling and in being. That is, the Word is telling us to be like the Father *and* the Word the Father *is* Love. And in much the same way, Jesus is both the intermediary between the Father and mankind as he transmits the Word that is Love and the literalization of the non-sacrificial attitude such Love requires. Girard's answer, then, is not the positioning of two complementary meanings, but a move toward collapsing them. According to Girard, the relationship between Son and Father is "a relationship of non-differentiated love" (270). And, recalling our discussion of Augustine, this relationship is logical and necessary.

Non-differentiation is precisely the mechanism Girard places against mimetic violence. Insofar as mimetic violence is based on a refusal of doubles to recognize themselves as such, as being in every sense that matters the same as the other, the Love of God reveals the truth behind the refusal. So when Girard writes that, like violence, "love abolishes difference," we understand this only with the provision that the two modes are completely incompatible (270). Mimetic violence, in the cultural setting, may institute a temporary reprieve from rivalry by laying difference itself onto the scapegoat. By making him or her or it bear the burden of difference, the community can *come together against* a literalization of the (often now only mythic) rivalry. The Christic innovation is the abolishing of all *coming together against*. That is, we might say that, in lieu of killing, of sacrificing, one need only hear the Word that erases difference and opens up the possibility of being like the Father. In Girard's terms, then, if the Father is to be a model, then the model is also undifferentiated Love that abides no rivalry.

This all sounds wonderful. The difficulty is that the economy of Love does not seem to be available, at least right now. In his discussion of the Johannine Logos, Girard addresses this problem directly and establishes its logic:

> The Johannine Logos is foreign to any kind of violence; it is therefore forever expelled, an absent Logos that never has had any direct, determining influence over human cultures. These cultures are based on the Heraclitean Logos, the Logos of expulsion, the Logos of violence, which, if it is not recognized, can provide the foundation of a culture. The Johannine Logos discloses the truth of violence by having itself expelled. (271)

What Girard argues is that the Word assumes (or has assumed) the position of expulsion itself. Given that one use of the scapegoat is the expulsion of difference, of mimetic rivalry by a society, the Word takes on its own agency (like the mother of the living child). The Word expels itself for the sake of denying any sacrificial reading of it. All of this is to say that Girard recognizes what he calls "the specificity of the Johannine Logos, which is to be an outcast" (272).[53]

If, as Girard writes, "Love is the only true revelatory power because it escapes from, and strictly limits, the spirit of revenge and recrimination," then this is only because Love has exiled itself from that economy (277). The Word stands outside mimesis. In Kristeva's terminology, the Word is abject. And it is to this notion we should now turn.

Early in *Powers of Horror*, Kristeva writes that the abject, "the jettisoned object, is radically excluded and draws me toward the place where meaning collapses" (2). Though perhaps too general, this working definition draws the contours of her object of study. And while the interests of our inquiry are less concerned with abjection, per se, than with the subject's relation to it, we should remember this formulation in particular when we return to place her with Girard. It is the latter part of the definition—the "place where meaning collapses"—that is perhaps most evocative, but we should begin where she does, with the split subject.

Kristeva claims (in good psychoanalytic manner) the split subject of language. Her innovation is to suggest that there is something prior to emergent subjectivity about which we can speak and through which much of what we have heretofore assumed about the subject of/in language becomes problematic. Kristeva formulates the split "[a]s if the fundamental opposition were between I and Other or, in more archaic fashion, between Inside and Outside" (7). If we are talking about a child, we might gloss this binary as the emergent subject-child and its mother. Insofar as the child recognizes that the mother is (belonging to the) Other, is both the object of desire (of the Father of Law in the Oedipal triangle which Kristeva does not abandon even as she critiques it) and that part of the child that is forever cut away and excluded from it, we can gather Kristeva's implications.

If the emergent subject is caught, as it were, between the solitary "I" of the ego and the Father who "has" the mother, then one cannot help but read here a private version of Girard's model in asmuch as the Father, the primary model after the subject's introduction to language, is recognized as "having" precisely that which the subject has always already (in the economy of the symbolic) been missing. Thus, the Father is the uncastrated exception to the phallic function. As Kristeva describes it, "[a] representative of the paternal function takes the place of the good maternal object that is wanting" (45). What we find, then, is an actual forsaking of the "archaic" Inside/Outside dichotomy—where that abjected *thing*, the mother, is a part of the child cut away in order for the child to join the symbolic order—for the desire of the model who is understood as possessing it all.

Of course, we are not only talking about children. That the above economy can be found in the social realm is evident in Kristeva' discussion of circumcision. What we find is shifting between the symbolic and the real. In other words, the real cutting-away, the primal trauma is positivized as a mark in the symbolic wholly aligning the subject with the Father and with his desire. Girard devotes an entire chapter to delineating precisely the adoption of the desire of the model by the subject as he enters into the symbolic structure called culture (299-325). And when Girard argues, "desire relieves its subject of an intolerable knowledge," it is exactly the knowledge of this primal cutting-away, honey of generation, the lack engendered at the very threshold of symbolization (303). This knowledge is forsaken for symbolic *meaning*.

Kristeva's whole project can be recognized in her insistence that, as what is primarily lacking shifts from one economy to the other, from the real to the symbolic, as it becomes an object of desire, it nonetheless also persists which is abject. And the abject is recognized as that which is fundamentally different, as the disgusting remainder that must be expelled in order to ensure the harmony of the symbolic order (both personally and culturally).

> Owing to the ambiguous opposition I/Other, Inside/Outside—an opposition that is vigorous but pervious, violent but uncertain—there are contents, "normally" unconscious in neurotics, that become explicit if not conscious in "borderline" patients' speeches and behavior. Such contents are often openly manifested through symbolic practices.... (7)

While Kristeva is addressing the state of patients, it is difficult not to recognize in her "contents" the conditions for Girard's sacrificial mechanism. Sacrifice should be read in these "symbolic practices" insofar as one might recognize in the borderline patient the societal crisis that engenders sacrifice as both the creation of a sacralized abject and its expulsion. What becomes apparent, and what explains Kristeva's interest in Girard, is that one finds the same behavior in both the personal and the cultural realms. Sacrifice is a reenactment of the primal separation through which the emergent subject already aligned itself with the Father and with his desire, in much the same way circumcision is a mark of alliance with God. Sacrifice is always an attempt at reconciliation.

The cultural and the personal develop in much the same manner. For Girard, the process is called hominization, the move from the animal to the human, which he defines as the collusion of "mimetic effects and a wholesale re-processing of symbols" (284). For Kristeva, the focus is the entrance of the child into the symbolic order, which is also, she claims, indicative of social involvement since "the subject of abjection is eminently productive of culture" (45). Important for both is what underlies the symbolic, what destabilizes it, and what can be called both the sacrificial object and the abject.

Of course, Kristeva's concern (like Girard's) is also finding a way by which the abject can be accounted for. And, as with Girard, Kristeva turns to the Christic innovation. Early in her book, Kristeva writes that the abject "finally encounters, with Christian sin, a dialectic elaboration, as it becomes integrated in the Christian Word as a threatening otherness—but always nameable, always totalizeable" (17). This Word, she suggests, is an attempt at purifying the abject. In the symbolic acting out of the Eucharist, for instance, in which the literalized Word is taken inside, "one might say that if the inside/outside boundary is maintained, osmosis nevertheless takes place between the spiritual and the substantial, the corporeal and the signifying—a heterogeneity that cannot be divided back into its components" (120). At the same time, however, the practice is always also one of expulsion. With Christ, who is the Word, one finds at once a body for the abject and the rationale for Christian confession.

In the first case, it is difficult to imagine Christ as abject, since he is by definition empty of what is disgusting, of what engenders violence. But, then again, moms are not inherently disgusting either. His place is as that which stands in the stead of what causes (or seems to cause) rivalry. That is, he can take up the position of the scapegoat. And this has certainly (and consistently) been one reading of the Passion. Where we find Kristeva leaving the sacrificial metaphor for Christ is when she maintains that "Christ alone, because he accomplished [the above] heterogeneity, is a body without sin. What others must do, *be-*

cause of their fault, is to achieve that sublimation, confess the part of themselves that rebels against divine judgment, a part that is innerly impure" (120, my emphasis). To be Christian is to assume abjection internally and personally. And to be Christ-like is to reach for that heterogeneity (Girard's non-differentiation) through expulsion that must be defined always as a self-expulsion. That is, one must confess.

If, as Kristeva claims, the Christian move is to internalize abjection and make each individual culpable (and so deny the scapegoat its efficacy), then, as with the Eucharist, we are witness to a transubstantiation. The abject, the defiled and defiling remainder of the real which must be expelled, is changed from Abominable Thing into sin. It is no longer substance, but act (119). For the Christian, then, "sin is an act and is proven to be within man's jurisdiction, within the scope of his own responsibility" (121). It is precisely through confession, through expulsion of/in words, that one gives up one's sin in order to approach the Word.

This new economy certainly seems different from Girard's. Where Girard has the Son-Word-God expelling itself, Kristeva seems to suggest that it is the self-expulsion of the abject that moves one toward the Christic. What reconciles this apparent disagreement is Kristeva's more explicit definition of sin:

> Meant for remission, sin is what is absorbed—in and through speech. By the same token, abjection will not be designated as such, that is, as other, as something to be ejected, or separated, but as the most propitious place for communication—as the point where the scales are tipped toward pure spirituality. (127)

The good Christian, like Christ, assumes the place of the abject as the abjected becomes…something else. The spirituality that comes from the assumption of one's abjection is the condition for language, or at least for communication, and it is by entering into the symbolic realm after having assumed the abject that one finds both one's place with/in the Word and one expels oneself. This is the other effect of confession.

> . . . Christians confess, hence avow[ing] their faith in Christ. . . . Already Christ has "confessed" in this way before Pontius Pilate. The avowal of faith is thus from the very start tied to persecution and suffering. This pain, moreover, has

> wholly permeated the word "martyr," giving it its basic, ordinary meaning, that of torture rather than testimony. Speech addressed to the other, not sinful speech but the speech of faith, is pain; this is what locates the act of *true communication*, the act of avowal, within the register of persecution and victimization. Communication brings my most intimate subjectivity into being for the other; and this act of judgment and supreme freedom, if it authenticates me, also delivers me over to death. (129)

Here is the true common ground for Girard and Kristeva. Kristeva makes explicit, through the double meaning of the word martyr, the substitution that allows the victimage mechanism to overpower the act of testimony: true communication. For both Kristeva and Girard, we should not read this type of martyr (of whom Christ is the supreme, perfect example) as a sacrifice, however much the victimizers might want to. The important effect is that the martyr, through words, through confession, expels herself inasmuch as she is free to assume her own death. This is the situation of the good mother caught in the Wisdom of Solomon.

If Kristeva and Girard differ, it is perhaps only in a manner of degrees. Girard assigns the renouncing of the victimage process, of mimetic rivalry and the rest, to the predicative Love, which is the Word that is God, as always exiled, as always out of reach. Kristeva allows both more and less. More, in that she finds reconciliation with abjection, its assumption and translation, in the language of confession itself. However, this reconciliation or assumption is always partial, always in the process of becoming:

> Power henceforth belongs to discourse itself, or rather to the act of judgment expressed in speech and, in less orthodox and much more implicit fashion, in all signs (poetry, painting, music, sculpture) that are contingent upon it. If such signs do not do away with the necessity for confession, they do spread out the logic of speech even to the most inaccessible folds of significance. (132)

With Kristeva, we are back once again with texts, though not as before. What Kristeva aims at is the knowledge such (special, literary, artistic) texts approach at the expense of meaning. This knowledge may be nothing less than the love Girard finds in the Word as Christ.

What both Girard and Kristeva call for, what makes them all but utopian, is a non-differentiated heterogeneity, a kind of sameness in difference, that would allow for communion with the divine while maintaining a radical difference, a that-which-is-in-me-but-not-of-me economy that is the complement to the Pauline "in the world but not of the world" motif. As we saw in the *Phaedrus*, love is intrinsic to me inasmuch as the object (that divinity, that special-sameness) that would allow an overall Oneness is missing. But I am capable of recognizing its potential in others, who can also recognize its potential, or latency, in me. Kristeva would positivize that lack as the abjected, exiled thing, which, in the best of all possible worlds, might be communally ingested and spit out. Sharing bread makes a family. The result is the kind of shifting from logical to temporal cause we saw before for the promise of a state (in all senses of the word) of "fraternal" love. What is fundamentally, even constitutively missing—what we will later call the object cause of desire—becomes a literalized, Word-made-flesh lost object of desire we need only claim and share. Notice the dropping of "cause" in this translation. Desire becomes, it seems, a cause (for) itself. The state of being human is fundamentally one of desiring, and desire itself is then recognized as the common thread that binds us together. As long as we keep desiring, that is.

As an example, consider the (terrible) Trey Parker film *Orgazmo*, about a young, displaced Mormon who becomes a porn star/super hero. When he is in Los Angeles trying to raise money for his big wedding and his betrothed is still in Utah, the engaged couple talks on the telephone, ending each conversation by saying "Jesus and I love you." Once the young woman surprises the hero at his doorstep and finds out that he has become an award-winning porn star, she is of course shocked and horrified until she finds out that *he participates only up to a point*. He performs for the plot, but when the actual sexual activity takes place, a "stunt" penis is called in, which apparently makes it all okay. The deferment of activity is, in this economy of love, precisely what allows for such (non)participation and what makes possible, when she says "Jesus and I love you," the hero's answer "Jesus and I love you, too." If both believe in that love, then "Heavenly Father" will forgive pretty much anything. Certainly, the hero does not violate the letter of the Law, but only sets the scene and provides the conditions and occasions for its breaking. And he is certainly in keeping with the spirit of the Law, since he is doing it all for love.

Girard's and Kristeva's arguments might be further fathomed if we realize that, for both, the formation of such a fraternity of love depends mostly on a change in the way one reads. For Girard, one must learn—or all must learn—to read the Logos instituted by Christ and come together under the banner of this new Love. Kristeva's whole book, while taking recourse to psychoanalysis and the Bible, is also a book about how to read good French literature, about how to read it confessionally and so participate in the sublime. In both, the relation between "love and the written" becomes an examination of sacrifice as the point where the symbolic enters into the field of being. That is, if being qua logical and necessary first (Girard's Christ and Kristeva's undifferentiated, presymbolic child) is broken down at the encounter of rivalry (mimetic or Oedipal), it is precisely at this juncture of being and becoming where the logical meets the temporal, that writing occurs as something other than a grocery list or receipt. Writing marks both a compromise and the site of a violence, the removal or exile of something later recognized as lost. The sublime is transformed into our recognition of the fact of such shearing and the gambit is that, by recognizing the constitutive lack inherent to all of us, a common ground is established which might be more trustworthy than any law that seeks to regulate the effects of that loss. Again, the spirit and the letter.

III. Love and Writing

Love is not the same thing as sex, of course. Both Girard and Kristeva ignore sex when reading love. So what about making love? Does it count? As love, or something else? Jacques Lacan claims that "love, in its essence, is narcissistic, and reveals that the substance of what is supposedly objectal—what a bunch of bull—is in fact that which constitutes a remainder in desire, namely, its cause, and sustains desire through its lack of satisfaction, and even its impossibility" (*Encore* 6). What could be more non-differentiated than narcissism? Love is the promise of sameness.[54] Such is good Plato and Longinus, and it is on this promise that Girard and Kristeva pin their hopes as they make moves toward a social order of the exiled.

Consider, though, Kierkegaard's description of and excuse for jilting his Regina in *Fear and Trembling*. Certainly, one cannot say for certain that he did not love her. Kierkegaard claims over and over that he did. He jilted her *because* he loved her. In fact, Kenneth Burke reads Kierkegaard as writing to transform his caddish behavior into something noble, even transcendent. The question, of course, is how to do that trick.

Like Girard and Kristeva, Kierkegaard also takes recourse to the Bible in order to make sense of love. In his case, the passage under consideration concerns the Ahkedah, the Binding of Isaac. Burke points to Kierkegaard's "psychologizing" of the story in order, by analogy, to excuse his own behavior toward Regina. Kierkegaard's reading is thus:

> He climbed Mount Moriah, but Isaac understood him not. Then for an instant he turned away from him, and when Isaac again saw Abraham's face it was changed, his glance was wild, his form was horror. He seized Isaac by the throat, threw him to the ground, and said, "Stupid boy, dost thou then suppose that I am thy father? I am an idolater. Dost thou suppose that this is God's bidding? No, it is my desire." Then Isaac trembled and cried out in his terror, "O God in Heaven, have compassion upon me. God of Abraham, have compassion upon me. If I have no father upon earth, be Thou my father!" But Abraham in a low voice said to himself, "O Lord in Heaven, I thank Thee. After all it is better for him to believe that I am a monster, rather than that he should lose faith in Thee." (*Rhetoric of Motives* 246)

Burke then considers Kierkegaard's personal additions to the narrative—the wild behavior Abraham performed in order to exculpate God—in terms of Kierkegaard's motivation to excuse his behavior toward Regina. Obviously, Abraham loves Isaac. But we should also notice peculiarities in Kierkegaard retelling. Abraham says that he is not Isaac's father, but an idolater. Isaac's father is presumably the father who worships God. This is apparently why Isaac can call out to the "God of Abraham" even though Abraham has, by his own words, denied his allegiance. But, of course, Abraham is really still loyal to God and is, in fact, so loyal that he is willing to become an object of fear and hate for his son in order to free God of that burden. Recalling the earlier discussion of the two mothers and Solomon, Abraham's actions are reminiscent of the real mother's, inasmuch as Abraham assumes the place of causality. Abraham becomes both the despised object of his son and, by saying "it is my desire," assumes the place of the secret desire of God as cause, evidenced in the last bit of the quoted section as Abraham speaks *to himself to God*. Abraham "said to himself, 'O Lord in Heaven....'" The question is: what does this have to do with reconciling Kierkegaard's love for Regina with his actions?

The answer posited by Burke is that, by removing any possibility of "having" Regina in the present (she has, for instance, married by this time), he is able to extend the "getting" indefinitely. That is, "by perpetual courtship [writing such things, in Kierkegaard's case] he is forever getting her while forever not getting her, renunciation and advance being fused in the one attitude" (251). How is the continual courtship attained? By being a cad.

> For if this "knight of faith" would court in terms of the infinite, it follows that he would court eternally, in perpetual repetition. Here would be the motive of the dialectician, of Socratic erotic. . . . But if one would court forever, whereas the object of one's courtship is not only willing to yield, but even becomes importunate in yielding, then the goodly dialectician must supply resistances of his own, from within himself, out of his own "inner check," and by setting up a situation, both emotional and practical, that would restore the necessary distance. (249)

It would be misleading to assume that this "inner check" is some inner belief of Kierkegaard's that he does not deserve Regina's love. Rather, the point Burke is making is that, in order to sustain love indefinitely, to keep desire at a particular distance in order to maintain the status quo for both Kierkegaard the man and Kierkegaard the writer/thinker (they are, in this economy, pretty much the same), he must jilt once, then court perpetually. And he courts in writing. So when Burke writes that, in Kierkegaard's retelling of the Isaac story, "though there is a questionableness here on one level, there is extremely revealing honesty on another," we recognize that the *questionableness* is any claim that Kierkegaard's writing is an examination or exegesis of the Bible passage (247). His *honesty*, however, becomes apparent when we perceive the innovation in the story as a mark of something else. For Burke, this something else is motive; for us, it is the play of desire across the written.

We might then read Kierkegaard's initial behavior as, in Lacanian terms, castration qua "the sign with which an avowal dresses itself up, the avowal that jouissance of the Other, of the body of the Other, is promoted only on the basis of infinity" (*Encore* 7). That is, jouissance (an enjoyment) is both a response to and a condition of repetition, and castration in this case is a refusal of impossible satisfaction. Loss is the mechanism by which Regina might be transmuted into an ultimate, separate Other. Thus, it is a self-castration. The paradox is that, by the avowal that sexual rapport with the Other is impossible—life with Regina was impossible *before* he broke it off with her, obviously, assuming that there is a motive for the act—such castration is also the only means through which Kierkegaard can keep enjoying her (as Other) through repeating the break *as something else.*

Burke calls this something else "perpetual courtship," thus demonstrating the positivization of loss in the infinite. It is not surprising that Kierkegaard would designate this situation as the Absurd. However, if Kierkegaard's behavior can be understood in terms of castration, we also find within it the seeds of (non) sacrifice. Kierkegaard himself assumes the place of the exiled object; Regina loves him, so he must become unlovable, expellable. What should be clear is that he must assume exile in order to keep enjoyment qua jouissance going *for himself.* In the face of the perceived impossibility of sexual rapport (Regina qua "real woman" cannot do it for him), he leaves to keep desire alive, transforming only later his (caddish) act into a (noble) cause. The result is that Regina, contained in a kind of stasis of loss, becomes the big-O-Other to which Kierkegaard might make every address. He writes precisely because she is unavailable and hence eternally lovable. Abraham, in the new version of the story, misrecognizes his own lack of faith for a lack in God (how can there be a people if the child is killed before he can reproduce?) and so assumes the place of what God is missing: a cause. Abraham pretends that he is sacrificing Isaac for himself and, by pretending, assumes the place of what is absent from God's demand: a reason or cause for the sacrifice. Another way of saying this is that, by providing a slipshod motivation for the potential slaying, Abraham gives up his own desire to found a people so that God would not have to support that burden. Abraham assumes the place of what must be missing: the evil intent to kill Isaac. That he lies by doing so should remind us that the real mother of the Solomon story also lies. The difference is that, where the mother is saving a child, Abraham is out to save God.

Kierkegaard misperceives his own castration (the missing cause of his desire in the presence of the "real woman") as a fundamental lack in his Other. Just as in the story Isaac is aligned with God as that part that must be sacrificed, Regina-the-woman is remade as the Other to whom Kierkegaard might make perpetual love. Burke claims that Kierkegaard, through the Isaac story (and the subsequent breast parable), seeks to transform the particular instance (his actions) into something transcendent and universal, an ultimate cause. We might say, then, that what one loves is repetition *taken as a whole* as the fantasy or dressing-up that covers over lack. What one *enjoys*, though, is repeating.

Lack and repetition have something to do with the written, of course. For Plato, misrecognition is the key to love, it seems, and with Longinus the claim is made for that same misrecognition (the image *seems* to appear, etc.) as constitutive of the sublime in language. That sublime stands separate from both the audience and the author; both experience it as external and extrinsic, which it must be if mortals are going to approach something of divinity.

Girard makes a similar move, first positing an object of contention for two parties who are resisting their identicalness and so are caught in rivalry, then reading the Word-cum-Love as the shared but extrinsic (exiled) ground for commonality. We should note here a peculiar movement of the object. Where the first object of contention drops away as rivalry takes over its own cause, the object returns as something rarified, translated (in all senses) into a separate, sublime guarantee. Translation is, of course, also interpretation, and Girard's process is primarily a hermeneutic one based on the assumption of positivized lack, the self-exiled (non) sacrificed One. Once the One of Christian Love is set, everything else refers to or can refer to it. The temporal (narrative) becomes part of the ultimate (logical) cause. As with Augustine, then, Christ is the Word and everything refers to the Passion as a ground pretending to be an event. That is, the Passion (as *the* act of love) is treated as a logical first cause to which everything prior refers (typology) and everything after points (being Christ-like).

Kristeva follows the themes of exile and translation in her notion of the assumption of abjection cum sin and its translation as prayer into language. "Christians," she writes, "confess, hence avow[ing] their faith in Christ" and "speech addressed to the other, not sinful speech but the speech of faith, is pain; this is what locates the act of *true communication*, the act of avowal, within the register of persecution and victimization" (129). It is difficult not to recognize this avowal as the mark of castration discussed above. An elaboration of the relation of pain and persecution as jouissance will be proffered in the next chapter, but what should be noted here is that Kristeva sets up an economy that moves our discussion from reading/experiencing to actual production, to speaking and to writing. For Kristeva, one speaks the abject. And one speaks it over and over and over.

This is exactly what Kierkegaard does. Apologia is confession (as Augustine knew), but not simply that. In Kierkegaard's apology, in his additions to the Isaac story in particular, the missing cause of his behavior—his act—is totalized into an Other cause registered as the first. Far from excusing "bad behavior," Kierkegaard is concerned with displacing the act itself. That is, misrecognizing the substantive paucity inherent to the act of caddish behavior (the missing object-cause), Kierkegaard retroactively translates the event into an appeal to the Other that can (and must) be repeated. He assumes the place of the exiled in order to, as my own father would say, "keep on keeping on." And here we find the proper place of writing as a continual appeal to the Other that both covers over the lack that constitutes the act—its fundamentally contingent nature—and reveals its mechanism in/as necessary repetition. Writing is a way of amplifying the gap in the written (as that essential, formal aspect of which all writing shares) while trying at the same time to cover over the gap by shifting from the temporal to the logical, from narrative to ultimate terms. Both Plato and Longinus insist on the ultimate, and Girard and Kristeva hide the ultimate cause by invoking its exile, abjection, turning lack into a loss, a sacrifice we can talk about.

4 Nothing But the Effects of Those Instances of Saying

The previous chapters began with certain tropes—Greek and Christian Love—and traced their function as replacements for a missing cause. Because the cause (for community and attraction) is missing, one cobbles a signifier that first stands in for that fundamental antagonism between lack (of a signifier) and its experience as a positive event.[55] Eventually, through a process best called dialectical, one transcends the particular to the universal, the infinite, the ultimate. The paradox is that, in the substitution of this (or any) signifier for the missing cause, in covering-over the substantive lack, that *made* master signifier also has the function of re-presentation in the sense that it sustains lack as a driving motive, thus insuring the continuance of desire, its play in confession and, indeed, in all writing. Writing is thus always an interpretation of/intervention in the substantive lack, a way of assigning meaning to what was, before, an unsignifiable, indecipherable event.

Interpretation, of course, needs a referent. And often—as with Girard, Kristeva, and Kierkegaard—referents are other texts. The mistake, or rather, the misrecognition that allows for the classical sort of interpretation (discovery of the meaning) is often the assumption of some fundamental, ultimate truth to which even the previous texts must be referring. The result is an amalgam of various texts linked together afterward through a common trope recognizable as such only when we realize that that trope is a stand-in for the metonymy of desire looking for its cause.

As an extreme example, consider such "research" into first causes in the Chariot-of-the-Gods kind of anthropology popular some years ago that seeks the single ancient society that can account for pyramid building, etc. around the world. In order for this sort of thinking to continue, what must remain unrecognized is that the *search* for some primary human society indicates a particular orientation toward desire. Instead of asking "What sort of ancient society can account for pyramids?" or even "Was there a first, global civilization?", we might ask why pyramids might be appealing as a structure. Even better, we should investigate why the assumption of a primary human society is appealing and wonder for whom this fantasy works and what desire it addresses. One point not to be lost is that, for those who research ancient aliens, say, the pyramids throughout the world are read as a question themselves. Pyramids create a space that history is conjured up to fill.

Following the trope by assuming Love as the answer allows Girard to plug the hole, to rectify the antagonism, in text/culture/history by making the Word identical with the transcendental Event, thereby retroactively turning the Greeks almost (but not quite) Christian.[56] His is not necessarily a poor move, as long as we recognize in it something sublime, Burke's "extremely revealing honesty." By *making meaning* in this way, Girard is able to tender a signifier that can claim truth status: the trope that God is, after all, Love. However, with such shifting from the temporal to the logical sphere comes the replacement of contingency with necessity, metonymy with metaphor. After accepting Girard's interpreted truth as *the* truth of scripture, all of history becomes the journey toward realizing that truth as both efficient and final cause.

If, however, we recognize that cause may in fact be (re)constructed after its ostensible effect—as the rabbis indicate when they stress the priority of interpretation—then it is also possible to read Love as a product as well. Our difficulty becomes, then, one of finding a way to address causation without positivizing (or humanizing) it while at the same time allowing the possibility of saying *something particular* about a subject. That is, given the problems we have noted above, can we still talk about history?

I. Contingency and History

> *In effect . . . alone among all to affirm itself as historical, in never propagating myth, midrash represents a primary mode of which modern historical criticism could well be only the bastardization. For if it takes the Book literally, it is not in order to make it the bearer of more or less pat-*

> ent intentions, but because of its signifying collusion taken in its materiality . . . to draw another statement from the text: nay, to imply in the text what it itself neglected.
>
> —Jacques Lacan

Lacan makes a case for imagining history as that which surrounds the missing cause. If midrash, as he says, is historical, it is so in that it does not maintain the common tropes discussed earlier. These tropes—read above as myth—are at best a supposed moral of the story and at worst the assumption that every story has a moral, that each story contains in it an intrinsic kernel of truth that is, really, a reference to an extrinsic, prior truism. Midrash avoids such assumption(s) by positing interpretation as a contingent collusion of the oral and the written, as construction instead of an excavation, as something that takes place in time: right now. This temporal dimension is one way of aligning the rabbinic with the rhetorical against the philosophical. And, as we saw in the second chapter, though midrash is interpretation, it is also writing.

From Lacan's explanation, we should draw two points:

1. The word "literally" here means consideration at the level of the letter, what we would call a close reading; this is not reading for metaphor as some symbol, type, or spirit of meaning, but a kind of exaggerated literality.
2. Such a writing of history draws "another statement" from its subject. Instead of simply offering up a new subject of meaning,[57] these writings indicate the tripartite state of the subject: the Lacanian dictum that a signifier is a subject for another signifier.

The result is that, instead of assuming the sacrosanct state of the subject (of study, say), midrashic (and psychoanalytic) history demonstrates the construction of the subject as the link between or among signifiers and the contingent nature of the subject, depending as it does on the matrix surrounding it.

As an example, consider classic Freudian word association. Where the analysand would create chains of words following an "inner logic" of sounds, cultural associations, etc. that illustrate both metaphoric substitution (at the level of pairs) and metonymic play (as the chain quickly becomes potentially infinite), the analyst is less interested in what words are proffered by the analysand than in those spaces between the words. What magical operators force one to connect *boat*, say, with *water, oar, sail*, or any number of other words?[58] The missing cause thus operates despite the fact that it is absent and, often by the sheer weight of such demonstration, the analysis is able to help reconstruct her missing desire. What must be stressed here, though, is:

1. the truth of the subject's desire is overdetermined by language in that she cannot help speaking it, and
2. this desire is re-constructed and is not assumed to be original. What comes to light after interpretation does not necessarily bear complete resemblance to what we would hypothesize existed before the interpretation.

In a sense, of course, it is the denial of any "original meaning" that actually allows for interpretation. If one cannot say anything certain about the intention of an author, for instance, one can nonetheless say *something* about the intentions of a text, with the caveat that the "contingent" nature of the subject is not read as "arbitrary." A text (a dream, a book, even word-association) cannot say everything, but is the condensation and displacement of latent content warped by/in desire; the "truth" of a text is called a *truth* only insofar as it stands in the place of what cannot be spoken, the absent cause of desire, and is the locus around which the signifiers (images, words) congregate. Thus, we say that a given subject condition is contingent, not arbitrary, since it is constrained or determined/defined by its position among the field of signifiers. Arbitrariness would stress the accidental nature of a supposed cause over the concrete effect(s) under investigation. And an interpretation cannot say "anything at all" about its subject; it is constrained by both manifest content (what is actually on the page; Ophelia was not married to Hamlet) and by its hermeneutic apparatus.[59]

In Freudian dream interpretation, the understanding is that latent content qua the experiences and frustrations of real life *and* the unspeakable cause becomes, through the dream work, the manifest content that is the dream proper. Much of analysis is the unknotting of the dream work to "get at" the latent content that seems to trouble the analysand, to separate out the day residue and to get at the cause. Of course, one can readily see the appeal of applying these analytic techniques to other manifest content: histories, novels, movies, and poems. What often goes unnoticed, however, is that the analytic process does not mimic the dream work itself; it is not a back-engineering project.

Rather, in its attempt to reveal "the cause" of a dream, analysis makes all sorts of assumptions, which are themselves based on its particular mode of interpretation. The result is that one cannot say with complete certainty that the narrative produced at the end of an analysis bears complete resemblance to the latent content. The latent content qua cause is lost to us. At the same time, it would be difficult to argue that what is produced by analysis has no meaning or no effect on the analysand at all.

What is brought forward by analysis is the constitution of (a) cause after the fact. That is, after the fact of there being an effect. And this "cause" is really an insinuation of another signifier or knot of signifiers. That is, the symptom itself. Thus, Lacan speaks of midrash *implying* "in the text what it itself neglected." The act of interpretation—or the act of writing anything at all—is not simply an inference gleaned from an existing text or life or real world, but rather a forcible exchange of one symptom for another. In analytic practice, the *implying* would be the intervention of the analyst. For this reason, Lacanian analysis does not assume "recovered memories" as facts. One may have been abducted by aliens, but any memory of the experience is not nearly conclusive evidence that it actually happened.

The point is that trauma qua cause is not the event itself, but that something that is missing for which the event comes to function as a placeholder. Thus, a person may develop a symptom many years after an event has taken place. History in such cases must be read as addressing the present, not the past. Put slightly differently, the event *as traumatic* becomes an object called into being for some current (condensing, displacing) function.

Shifting registers for a moment, doesn't something like this appear in the academy? In the literary canon, consider the introduction of William Blake. Until the 1950s, he was an oddity studied by only a very few specialists. He entered the canon then not because his works were hidden by malicious rivals or hoarded by greedy scholars, but because we needed him *now* as a powerhouse Romantic poet/artist. For our story of literary epochs, we needed the transition figure. It is not a happy accident that his visual sense and writing happen to appeal to our own sensibilities. It was necessary for his recovery. In the same vein, more contemporary moves to restore, for instance, certain women writers to their proper places in anthologies would not be revisions of history nor marks of conspiracy or of the paucity of the canon as much as an admission that we need them now for our own work and for our own purposes. The fact that we assume that the newly discovered lack (of a transition-poet for the Romantics) is a loss in history demonstrates the Lacanian motifs that "the truth arises from misrecognition" and of the future-anterior, the "what will have been." William Blake had to be *constructed* as he was recovered. Or we could say that Blake was invented in the 1950s.

II. Cause and Trauma and Narrative

People do History precisely in order to make us believe that it has some sort of meaning. On the contrary, the first thing we must do is begin from the following: we are confronted with a saying, the saying of another person who recounts his stupidities, embarrassments, inhibitions, and emotions. What is it that we must read therein? Nothing but the effects of those instances of saying.

—Jacques Lacan

A psychoanalytic approach to history is quite different from what people are likely to do in popular biographies or even history departments. One might contend that, by foreclosing the possibility of available meaning in the study of the past, Lacan is to a significant extent denying the efficacy of any number of disciplines that claim to say something about what it means to be human. A response to such a critique would be that, where Lacan is in fact less interested in meaning as a constructed patchwork of signifiers—a narrative—claiming to be true, he does offer a replacement: knowledge. Knowledge is exactly what the analyst is after. We should recall the discussion of analysis above and recognize that what is at stake in dream analysis and in word association is not a meaning produced by the words but rather the knowledge they are both revealing and trying to cover over. Knowledge is, in this schema, exactly that which cannot be articulated; knowledge is nothing but acknowledgement of the formation of a lack.[60]

In her gloss of Freud's *Moses and Monotheism*, Cathy Caruth assumes equity between histories—or at least this supposed history Freud produced—and narrative. Indeed, people have tended to read Freud's work as a creative, even literary text more than any historical account of an actual people. But as a narrative first, certain possibilities for its reading are opened that would be denied by the straight assumption of a referential, this-is-what-happened-then simple history. Of course, most all histories are narrative. They often have plot, for instance. What is significant is that, when one's primary concern is less the supposed truth of a particular referent (a date, say, or a name) and more the organizational structure that narrative as a particular kind of writing *is*, certain gaps and contradictions become apparent that may lead to anOther understanding. Jean Baudrillard writes:

> What is involved . . . is not a "liberation" of language [that is, not the removal of all referent, or language as sheer play], nor its dislocation as an effect of unconscious contents [not that the unconscious does the writing], but an extreme, accidental form in which language seems to wish to go beyond its intentional operation and get caught up in its own dizzying whirl. (37)

Language, he indicates, has its own agency, is Other. And writing, on the way to saying something meaningful about a particular subject, may produce—or, rather, implicate—something else besides. This *something else* has little to do with authorial intention (but perhaps everything to do with what Kenneth Burke calls motive) and may take an accidental (or, better, contingent) form.[61]

For these reasons, Caruth reads Freud's text in terms of Freud's writing of it. She seeks "the effects of those instances of saying" rather than the meaning Freud might seek to produce. Freud explains the circumstances for the text's production in introductions, notes, and in letters, and Caruth reads these circumstances as part of the primary text, which of course they are under this reading paradigm. We will consider the nature of narrative later, but what is useful now is Caruth's understanding of trauma as both departure and return. She writes: "Centering his story in the nature of the leaving, and returning, constituted by trauma, Freud resituates the very possibility of history in the nature of a traumatic departure. . . .What does it mean, precisely, for history to be the history of a trauma?" (15). In Freud's particular argument, the answer is something like the combining of what may or may not be "historical" (in the straight referential sense; the murder of one Moses, the introduction of another, and their combination) into a common narrative that at once gives a history (a past) and founds a people (a present as an unwritten but indicative future in the myth). This is what allows Freud to write that Moses invented the Jews, without bothering to indicate which Moses applied for the patent. That is, Moses is a place-holder, a signifier without a particular signified except an excess, a trauma, something Caruth calls "a latency" (17).

The latent character of trauma, the fact that it happens too soon for signification and is committed to returning as bits of the real-cum-signification (symptoms, holocausts) explains both how Freud's work can be considered historical (it marks the contours of an event that cannot be spoken) and how Freud's writing as a return to trauma (his political and personal situation) supports the notion of the return of the repressed (and allows for the understanding of trauma as Baudrillard's "event" and its writing as being the enactment of what both Lacan and Lyotard call the future anterior, the "what will have been"[62]). Perhaps it would be useful to remember here that trauma is often posited as being universal. Chaitin writes that trauma is "the unassimilable kernel at the heart of human experience, and the contingent, the only haven for human subjectivity" (9). Particular traumas are, well, particular, but trauma as the mark of entering into language (and culture) is what Julia Kristeva is concerned with when she discusses the abject as the remainder of what cannot be symbolized, what Chaitin writes of in his discussion of the lost object and the death drive and what Lacan considers the object cause. Freud could not seem to give up his book at precisely the time he was preparing for his own departure "to die in freedom" (Caruth 23). That is, as Caruth writes in her gloss of Lacan's reading of the burning child dream, "the gap between the accident [for us, Freud's situation] and the words . . . produces a significance . . . that must be read in the relation between the chance event and the words it calls up" (101). There is a gap between the event and the language apparently provoked by the event that maintains the incommensurate nature of the event/word relation. It is important to recognize here that something is missing, namely a signifier for what is revealed in the gap, which becomes apparent only in the particular, contingent context. Thus, the traumatic event (that which cannot be spoken) is imminently productive of words; since one can never quite "say" the event, one is left with always *trying* to say it.[63] And these instances of saying are in fact the traces of what cannot be spoken, but is nonetheless always spoken about. Put another way, there is no *sein* without *dasein*, as long as the "being there" is projected from the future into the past following the logic of "what will have been." The act of saying is in effect the pursuit of the—by definition, missing, formal—cause of the event *becoming significant*. The result of this lack of cause is precisely the desire or need to produce new signifiers which are never quite right, are always contingent on/in the present, but which nonetheless trace the condition for—and the cause of—writing.

III. Temporal Cause, Logical Cause, and Something Else

One result of treating trauma as a cause that cannot be apprehended directly is that, when its effects are registered, counted, and deciphered—that is, when the trauma is pinned to an event—something seems to happen to time. Where there was nothing/lack/formative trauma, there are then registered effects, and then there is reconstructed trauma which we cannot claim is original but which we nonetheless treat as a cause.[64] Thus, the cause (the reconstructed trauma) follows the effects, as the contingent thing (happening, accident, whatever) registers as the necessary cause (the traumatic event).

One way of addressing the logic of the first cause that is both formative and contemporary is actually very old. Aristotle's Mover functions as the pivot for action and time while always remaining outside of them; it is not a temporal process, but a logical relation. We should remember here our discussion in the first chapter of the possibility of shifting between logical and temporal causation. Logical causes are principles, and it should be clear that it is possible to treat trauma as such a principle, too. Principles exist prior to any motive, act, or event. They simply are, and in this sense *are* ahistorical constants. This is their latent character. But, as we saw, there are dangers when one shifts from the logical (which is necessary) to the temporal (which is contingent). The logically necessary (the *all* of the masculine position) does not completely map to the temporally contingent (the *not-all* of the feminine), and problems can arise when some thing that is purely formal (the necessary, primary lack/trauma) is conflated with the contingent event that covers over that lack. This conflation is precisely what Caruth points to when she says that the event "happens too soon" for symbolization.

What should be clear is that not every horrible event is traumatic. Only those events that functionally indicate lack in the symbolic by becoming signifiers for that lack attain the status of trauma.[65] So one strategy for reading and hearing language responding to trauma is to pay close attention to what is not being spoken but what is nonetheless being spoken about. Clearly, one goal of analysis is the analysand's uttering of that previously unspoken (and unspeakable) signifier. Indeed, one objective is actually to produce a signifier for what had none before. What remains unclear, though, is how that signifier can come into being (so to speak) after the work of analysis or writing or reading. That is, how might cause appear after its effect?

Slavoj Žižek offers an example of this apparent paradox in the form of the joke about the conscript

> who tries to evade military service by pretending to be mad. His symptom is that he compulsively checks all the pieces of paper he can lay his hands on, constantly repeating: "That is not it!" He is sent to the military psychiatrist, in whose office he also examines all the papers around, including those in the wastepaper basket, repeating all the time: "That is not it!" The psychiatrist, finally convinced that he really is mad, gives him a written warrant releasing him from military service. The conscript casts a look at it and says cheerfully: "That *is* it!" (*Sublime* 160)

The warrant finally produced has the structure of an object that retroactively causes the symptom. The symptom as repetition and failure—looking at every piece of paper in hope of finding "it"—makes sense only in terms of what it ultimately produces. The second point not to be missed is that everyone around the conscript makes the mistake of not realizing how they are already inscribed in the symptom. That is to say, truth arises from misrecognition. Assuming a properly scientific, objective position outside of the game is precisely what leads to their culpability in the production of the object-cause.

If what we are searching for is cause after the fact, the object produced in its enunciation, Caruth indicates that we might find the cause by looking closely at the effects—the symptoms, the sayings—in terms of aspects of their apparent structure. And with many texts, chief among such aspects is narrative structure.

IV. Narrative, Lack, and Discourse

Reality is approached with the apparatuses of jouissance...
[and] there's no apparatus other than language.

—Jacques Lacan

Ivan Marcus writes that medieval Jewish chronicles are "products of coherent religious imaginations" (42). Medieval chroniclers, he suggests, were not interested in presenting flat factual information for its own sake. Rather, writers more likely viewed the events they depicted through the prism of their own agendas. Events were often included only if and when they jibed with the focus of the project at hand, there was in every case a motive behind the writing, and historical accuracy was always servant to cultural expedience and the necessities of belief. "Medieval chronicles are, in this sense, fictions: imaginative reorderings of experience within a cultural framework and system of symbols" (42). What Marcus calls for is a reevaluation of such texts in light of their literary/structural qualities in order to grapple with the culture beneath the fictions. By displacing questions as to the actual historical accuracy of the narratives, we may approach the literary aspects of given works in their own terms and address the motives they represent. And what we are after here is what we can know of the (sometimes repressed) motives presented by such fictions as grounding for the form the work takes. That is, given that the work is fiction, why must it be *just* so? What job does narrative do, and what is this particular narrative talking *about*?

Accepting that these narratives can be approached as fictions, then, the object at hand is one such writing, *The Chronicle of Solomon bar Simson*, written about a few events of the First Crusade. Our particular focus is the portion of the Chronicle dealing with the acts of homicide and suicide in Mainz as they are presented in specific terms of sacrifice. The goal here is to pinpoint what an ostensibly literary and religious narrative about historical events might suggest that the events themselves could not. Which is to say, how might the very *narrativity* of the writing implicate a lack in representation and so rise to the level of an *act*? That we will be adopting a Lacanian framework for our discussion in no way forecloses other approaches, but rather opens for specific consideration what might usually be taken for granted: the fantasy structure intrinsic to fictions.

The reasons for such a narrow focus are several. The Mainz portion contains the meat of the Chronicle; well over half of the narrative is concerned with the events there. And other sources, both Christian and Jewish, mostly corroborate the historical record offered in the narrative. Also, limiting our discussion to these sections allows for some approximate dating, since they are the only parts of the narrative that are likely the product of one writer (though even this is problematic). Finally, the Mainz sections of the narrative, taken as a unit, comprise a literary-religious text of some complexity, and we will do well to unravel something of its promise.

The Chronicle begins with a gloss of the persecutions in three Rhenish communities, then focuses on the events in Mainz in detail. Generally, the history offered in the narrative is substantiated by other Jewish and Christian sources. Where Bar Simson's account differs from the Christians', most contradictions are geographical or statistical and may be chalked up to confusion of names, etc., or obvious polemic (Eidelberg 17-18). At the very least, though, both Christian and Jewish sources recognize the events at Mainz as marking unprecedented action on the part of the besieged Jews. The Christian Albert of Aix, for instance, wrote:

> the Jews, seeing that their Christian enemies were attacking them and their children, and that they were sparing no age, likewise fell upon one another, brother, children, wives, and sisters, and thus they perished at each other's hands. Horrible to say, mothers cut the throats of nursing children with knives and stabbed others, preferring them to perish thus by their own hands rather than to be killed by the weapons of the uncircumcised. (Krey 55)

Albert condemned the attacks, and it is difficult not to recognize the contempt he had for the persecuting Crusaders, calling them "brutish and insensate animals" (56).

As far as the dating of our portion of the Chronicle is concerned, we can estimate that it was composed around the middle of the twelfth century, though there are some anachronisms that might place it later, at least in part. Ivan Marcus apparently dates the chronicle earlier, writing that the Bar Simson and two other narratives "were written in the early twelfth century shortly after the events they portray" (41). The difficulty is that the narrator places himself in 1140 (Eidelberg

55). An added problem is that the portions dealing with self-immolation and the prayers of dead souls indicate the influence of *Sefer Hasidim*, dating the chronicle even later, probably after the second half of the century (16). This point of assigning a later date to the writing of the Chronicle is made to stress the basic supposition that the Chronicle is not in itself an eyewitness account responding immediately to the energy of the times (though it may be based on the testimony of several witnesses), but a narrative composed after at least some time for reflection and designed to achieve a particular effect. That the Chronicle is in a general sense literary insofar as it represents an attempt at *creating* a detailed narrative for a *reason*.

This notion of creation is important. Whereas the common bumper sticker might claim "shit happens," we still make the fundamental assumption that events happen for reasons, through a relation of cause and effect which might be mapped and turned into a story. And though such a story is by definition a fiction, we cannot say that it is therefore not true (unless, of course, we are willing to say that there is nothing that is true).

For instance, we can say (without much fear of compromising our academic skepticism) that in 1095, Pope Urban II called for a Crusade against the Muslims who occupied so-called Christian lands in the east. His direct appeal reads thus:

> On this account I, or rather the Lord, beseech you as Christ's heralds to publish this everywhere and to persuade all people of whatever rank, foot-soldiers and knights, poor and rich, to carry aid promptly to those Christians and to destroy that vile race [Turks and Arabs] from the lands of our friends. I say this to those who are present, it is meant also for those who are absent. Moreover, Christ commands it. (Fulcher of Chartes 515)

In no way did he explicitly preach action against Jews. But apparently many Crusaders who answered his call recognized little difference between Jew and Muslim and ferocious attacks against Jews spread with the Crusaders march.

But this general mapping of cause and effect is contingent on a great many other fictions. First, we must recognize that Urban's appeal is made relative to his position both in Christian Europe and as a Christian. A Muslim obviously wouldn't have made such a call, nor would a Jew presumably care one bit about Arab incursions into Christian lands. And we should notice the assumption that these are Christian lands at all, a claim with which others certainly would (and did) disagree. Finally, we have to consider even our own understanding of the reactions to the call by the Pope, since it does not necessarily follow that an appeal to excise Muslims would lead to attacks on Jews. But it *is* apparent to us, since this is exactly what happened. The point is that narrative *as the chronicle of effects* is always produced after the fact. Any notion of cause and effect within a narrative is predicated upon the presumption of a time when one can understand the events from the perspective of what *will have happened*, what Jacques Lacan designates as the future anterior. In *Encore*, Lacan states unequivocally that "[e]very reality is founded and defined by a discourse" (32). That is, everything that can be spoken or written about, everything we would consider reality is determined precisely by the ability to speak and write it. There is no prediscursive reality. In one sense, then, what Lacan articulates is *the* mode of interpretation as narrative insofar as every narrative (in particular those purporting to present historical actions) both fictionalizes the events it presents and sustains them as/in reality.

The importance of the above formulation for our reading of the Chronicle is two-fold. First, this understanding supports Marcus' claim that we should approach such medieval writings as fictions, as "products of coherent religious imaginations." Secondly, an insistence on the narrative aspect of the text allows us to consider its relation to fantasy in its strict psychoanalytic sense.

Two complementary narratives structure the Mainz portion of the Bar Simson Chronicle. The first describes the political situation. As the invaders approach, the Jews of Mainz first elect elders who go to the city officials in order to purchase the safety of the Jewish community. The Jewish representatives are "respected by the local bishop" and are told to "bring all your money into our treasury. You, your wives, and your children, and all your belongings shall come into the courtyard of the bishop until the hordes pass by. Thus will you be saved" (Eidelberg 24). The bishop ultimately proves unwilling or unable to protect the Jews from the approaching Crusaders and the Jews are forced to take other action. This political narrative focuses on the leaders of each group, describing exchanges among men of power and offering what may be a fairly accurate representation of the social relations between the Jews and Christians living in the same community. Since Christians could not lend money for interest, for example, Jews often fulfilled the office and many stored their money in church treasuries (6). This is a point to which we will return later.

The second narrative tells of the events following the failure of the bishop to protect the Jews. The homicides and suicides of this portion mark a stark contrast to the preceding part; where the political narrative dealt with men of some power acting for the group in predictable ways, the martyrs are offered as "individual members, regardless of their power and authority, of a particular Jewish community" (Marcus 43-44). The narrative becomes scattered as the focus shifts from one individual or group to the next. The acts of homicide and suicide are unprecedented, shocking, and "the typological antecedents which are offered . . . are evoked in order to show how far they have been outstripped by present events" (45):

> Inquire and seek: was there ever such a mass sacrificial offering since the time of Adam? Did it ever occur that there were one thousand and one hundred offerings on single day—all of them comparable to the sacrifice of Isaac, the son of Abraham? ...Wilt Thou restrain Thyself for these things, O Lord? It was for You that innumerable souls were killed! (Eidelberg 33)

The first question is rhetorical; the obvious answer is no, there has never been such a mass offering. The next sentence, while seeming to repeat the former question, instead offers a precedent that is no precedent. Given that so many people died by their own or their parents' hands as an offering for God, how is this in any way comparable to the sacrifice of Isaac, which wasn't a slaughter at all, at least in kind?

The Chronicle frames the killings in terms of sacrificial offerings and calls to a precedent that obviously doesn't exist. The actors of the Chronicle actively and willingly assume their roles as offering—in particular killing their children in the manner of temple sacrifices (for instance, one mother catches the blood of her children in her sleeves just as a priest would process the blood offering; Eidelberg 25).[66] The emphasis here is on willingness and ritual. And we might actually understand the latter as predicated upon the former, insofar as ritual itself may be figured as the performative rules (usually based on precedent) for some sort of previous agreement toward action: I want to do this, so what is the best (most efficient, most effective) way to do it? What seems to be at stake is the willingness, even the eagerness of the people to engage in self-sacrificial activity. This takes us to its supposed precedent.

The focus on willingness does seem to jibe with the Binding of Isaac narrative, at least as represented by Rashi, whose Isaac realizes that he is to be slaughtered by his father as both father and son proceed up the mountain willingly, "with equal enthusiasm" (comment to 24.8, 234). But of course Isaac is not sacrificed. In fact, God specifically prohibits Abraham from harming Isaac, though Abraham is eager to at least give Isaac at least a little cut (comment to 22.12, 235). But outside of their shared willingness, how is the mass killing narrated by the Chronicle related to the aborted slaughter of Isaac at the level of an act? How can the Binding myth be offered as a precedent for the suicides and homicides when it is by example a disavowal of such an act? Abraham cannot slaughter Isaac, since such an act would negate God's promise of a people. We find the same concern in the Chronicle when one group of martyrs cries "Ah Lord God! Wilt thou make a full end of the remnant of Israel?" (Eidelberg 28). But where Abraham is stopped in time, the Jews of Mainz kill their children and themselves *because* God has demanded it (28). Despite the apparent contradiction, we are told to read these medieval actions as sacrifices of the same order. As we shall see later, such a problematic equivocation depends on a particular formulation of narrative in terms of fantasy. But in order to get at such a formulation, we might first look to another conflict, that between the political and martyrological which Ivan Marcus finds in the Chronicle itself.

To reconcile the opposition he perceives between the two aspects of the narrative, Marcus turns to a theory of paradigms offered by Thomas Kuhn and elaborated by Victor Turner. Paradigms, writes Marcus, "enable the same people to reorder the world they experience in different ways" (46). When one's basic circumstance changes, one is forced to shift one's world-view to a more accommodating perspective; once one assumes a radically new (social, symbolic) role, an accompanying reordering becomes necessary. The following is worth quoting in full:

> Thus, before the Jews "saw" that political action was futile, they behaved like medieval Jews and sought protection from their political rulers; after they interpreted political and military failure as the judgment of God, they reordered their worldview according to a new paradigm, the Temple cult. The same people lived in two cultural worlds because they processed

experience through two different cultural grids. The political narratives follow the Esther paradigm of political intercession in the Gentile court. When it becomes clear that there would be no Purim in Germany, the Temple paradigm takes over. Political leaders are replaced by lists of individual martyrs; the court is now the Temple altar; conventional collective Jewish-Christian relations become extraordinary acts of individual defiance which testify to the truth of Judaism and the falsehood of Christianity. (46)

The system that had served the Jews before (appeal and ransom) was not adequate to meet the new challenge, so they were forced to make a change at the level of basic understanding. As reasonable as this sounds, such a reduction does little to present the complexity of what the narrator of the Chronicle offers. According to Marcus, the Jews of Mainz are creatures of "two different cultural grids." And certainly we might understand that medieval Jews had both a secular profile and a strictly religious one. But it would be rash to equate the two cultural situations—the relatively free exchange between Christians and Jews before the riots and the closed religious life defined as distinctly Jewish both before and after the events— and the political action/martyrdom binary Marcus finds in the text. The former pair coexisted somewhat peacefully, were concurrent states, whereas the latter represents a temporal move as much as it does two separate paradigms. If the narrative itself is the concern, the question should not be what change in worldviews took place, but rather what effect is produced by the pairing, if not that of a founding, oppositional binary?

Of course, the binary itself is not so simple. Though Marcus makes a clear case for politics versus martyrology, it would be helpful to remember that the Jewish political situation is just as much a product of fundamental religious belief as the unprecedented later action. The Jews of Mainz are in the position of offering bribes and conferencing with bishops *because of* their religious difference (the Jews are the moneylenders, they need protection, etc.). If the Chronicle offers a "Jewish interpretation" of the events, then it would be prudent to focus on the narrative in terms of its Jewish*ness*. Being Jewish is integral to their situation; the Jews of Mainz are Jews by virtue of the very laws, rituals, and beliefs that support their later actions. Extrinsic pressures may define their status among the Christians (as moneylenders, as "killers of Christ"), but what we find in these terms is not another binary in place of the cultural grids. The intrinsic and extrinsic must be understood as consubstantial. The extrinsic Christian pressures are directly related to (even supported by) the intrinsic Jewishness of the protagonists of the narrative.

In psychoanalytic terms, before the events of the Crusade, the Jews of Mainz were perfectly willing to keep money for Christians, assume a place as reminders of the Passion of Christ, provide an economic or religious scapegoat, in essence sacrifice their own jouissance, their own enjoyment of/as a nation (a sacrifice which allows them a place in the symbolic order qua community) to the Other's desire. That is, the Jews may be willing to be the (deferred) object of the Other's desire, but not of his jouissance. They will forego self-governance, will give over whatever marks them as enjoying subjects for the sake of belonging, as long as the Christians do not gain any direct, final satisfaction from it. The point is maintenance, not satisfaction. Of this economy, Žižek writes:

> In the dialectic of Master and servant, the servant (mis)perceives the Master as amassing jouissance, and gets back (steals from the Master) little crumbs of jouissance; these small pleasures (the awareness that he can also manipulate the Master), silently tolerated by the Master, not only fail to present any threat to the Master but, in fact, constitute the 'libidinal bribery' which maintains the servant's servitude. (*Plague* 34)

This was essentially the relationship before the Crusade, a metonymy of exchange in order to maintain the status quo. And we link this metonymy with desire, since desire is "fundamentally caught up in the dialectical movement of one signifier to the next, and is diametrically opposed to fixation. It does not seek satisfaction, but rather its own continuation and furtherance . . ." (Fink 91). As long as the Mainz Jews keep offering their jouissance, everything is fine. But with the Crusaders we find something different. The Christians are no longer registering their relation to Jews at the level of desire. That is, the Crusaders are not asking that the Jews of Mainz give up their jouissance in order to find (or found) a place in the symbolic order we would call community, thereby continuing the secular/religious dialectic. In place of desire, the Crusaders register a demand. And what is this demand except that the Crusaders enjoy the Jewish jouissance, not its sacrifice? That is, the Crusaders' demand is for the supplemental jouissance set up in the above exchange, the "little crumbs" of Žižek's economy, which is in some sense the paradoxical enjoyment of the sacrifice of enjoyment—the jouissance inherent to the sacrifice of the servant qua the maintenance of a people. Desire has no object, but demand certainly does. This is the fantasy supported by the Crusaders' demand.[67] By offering only the options of conversion or death, the object of the Crusaders' demand is nothing other than the very Jewishness of their victims.

The Jews of Mainz are faced with the "forced choice" in its Lacanian formulation (*Four Fundamental Concepts* 212-213). Since the mugger's cry "Your money or your life" means that, either way, you have already lost your money, we might be tempted to read the Crusaders' demand thus: give up your difference or die. The innovation of the Jews' answer is that they do not recognize the demand in such terms. Since the demand is for their difference, for their Jewishness qua signifier that guarantees their place in the Other, the Mainz Jews are able to reformulate the supposed choice into something quite different. Through the cult of sacrifice, the Jews can have both (remain Jewish and die), and it is death as answer to the demand that re-founds their place in the symbolic order as community, though this time as martyrs. By killing their children and themselves, they are able to keep their Jewishness. The adults might die as Jews, but the children would be taken. This explains the special emphasis on the sacrificial killing of the children (the future of the people), so that they will not be reared as Christians. The children will remain Jewish as Jewish martyrs.[68] So what Marcus identifies as a full-on paradigm shift might be better rendered as changes in the extrinsic characteristics—a shift from desire to demand—so dramatic that this move forces a retreat even further inward, to the very essence of what it means to be Jewish.

We might now recognize that something comparable is happening with regards to the other conflict, the apparent disparity between the Binding of Isaac myth and the self-sacrifice of the Mainz Jews. At this point we should recall our insistence on the inherently narrative quality of the Chronicle, its dependence on discourse in order to sustain the reality it claims to report. All narratives, no matter how ancient or postmodern, are temporal (if only at the level of the sentence). That is, narrative depends on an accumulation, a building upon what has happened before and a belief that something more is always coming. In this sense, narrative contains both its past (as necessity) and its future (as potential). With regard to the function of this temporality,

Slavoj Žižek suggests that "*narrative as such* emerges in order to resolve some fundamental antagonism by rearranging its terms into a temporal succession. It is thus the very form of narrative which bears witness to some repressed antagonism" (*Plague* 10-11). Can the presence of narrative itself be the mark of the conflict narrative is supposed to hide? This seems counterintuitive, since the "antagonism" is really only made apparent by the attempt to resolve it. We will address this concern later, but our other problem is obviously the nature of this supposed antagonism.

We are still, after all, dealing with discourse, with (written) signs and their peculiar ordering (as narrative) to sustain something we have called reality. This reality is constructed and cannot, by definition, be all-inclusive. It is determined by what can be talked about, what can be represented. Moreover, reality (in a chronicle or in the world) is determined by the temporality inherent in representation and, since it is impossible to say everything at once, there must be something missing, if here only at the level of the sign. There is, after all, still the future which, however implicit in narrative, is rendered only as potential at any given point. We might then say that narrative at any particular moment is always insufficient, that its assumption of a future marks a fundamental lack and that the conflict between what it purports to sustain (a mechanics of the fantasy of completeness) and this lack (the impossibility of saying it all) gives impetus to the very *production* of narrative, both psychic and written. It is the site of this lack "at which, in every use of language, writing may be produced" (*Encore* 34).

We clearly find this concern with the future in the Binding myth. After stopping Abraham from slaughtering Isaac, God says, "For now I know that you are God-fearing, and you have not withheld your son . . . from Me" (Rashi et al. 22.12). Certainly, this cannot be read as implying that God didn't know beforehand. Rashi explains that the "now I know" should be read as: "From now on I have something with which to answer Satan and the non-Jewish nations who wonder what is the cause of my love for you. I have a justification that they see 'that you are God-fearing'" (commentary to 22.12, 236). Then Abraham names the site of the sacrifice "'Hashem Yireh, ["Hashem will see," that is, "Hashem will select and see fitting for Himself . . . to have offerings brought here"], as it is said this day . . ." (22.13). Rashi's explanation is involved:

AS IT IS SAID THIS DAY. That they will say of it in the days of future generations, "On this mountain, the Holy , Blessed is He, appears to his people. THIS DAY...refers to the days of the future, as does "until this day" which appears throughout Scripture. For all generations to come who read this verse apply "until this day" to the day in which they stand.

And the aggadic Midrash interprets our verse: "Hashem will see" this binding, to forgive Israel because of it every year, and to save them from punishment, so that it will be said, on this day, in all future generations, "On the mountain of God there *will be seen*" the ashes of Isaac still piled up, as if he had been actually sacrificed, for atonement on behalf of Israel. (Commentary to 22.13, 237, emphasis added)

The logic of the future anterior is explicit here. The sacrifice is to be treated as if it were *actually* sometime in the future. The Binding myth functions at once as a founding narrative of a people and a promise to those people that God "will see" the ashes of the sacrifice when *it will be* necessary. The promise is dependent on the potential future, the meaning as actual sacrifice is deferred, and the narrative itself is a mark of what will have been necessary. And this mark is precisely the lack discussed in the previously. The myth as narrative covers over its incompleteness through its structure as narrative, through the fantasy of completeness illustrated here as a trick of grammar.[69] Implicit in the apparent cause-effect relation of the myth is something else, what we might call an affect of discourse. We can approach this lack another way.

Narrative, by its nature, must keep moving in order to cover up what is always already missing from it. Another way of talking about this lack is in terms of symbolic castration, a cut in the signifying system that is by necessity always present (well, except for psychotics). But what can be said to be missing fundamentally? Or, rather, how might we figure a fundamental lack (one which is apparently pre-given—the "antagonism" above) when the cut is instantiated by the very process by which we try to cover it up? Žižek suggests:

> Let us imagine a situation in which the subject aims at X (say, a series of pleasurable experiences); the operation of castration does not consist in depriving him of any of these experiences, but adds to the series a purely potential, nonexistent X, with

respect to which the actual accessible experiences appear all of a sudden as lacking, not wholly satisfying. One can see here how the phallus functions as the very signifier of castration: the very signifier of the lack, the signifier which forbids the subject access to X, gives rise to its phantom. (*Plague* 15)

This phallic signifier, then, may be understood as *a priori* insofar as it by definition and in every case forecloses access to the object of desire (a wholly satisfying something: *a*) that paradoxically is engendered by the very search it frustrates. We might now understand the imperative to keep moving as a metonymy of desire, a shift from one small "x" to another in a futile attempt at laying hold of the "potential, nonexistent" final one. That we recognize this metonymy as a narrative—with an established *before* and a guaranteed *after*—indicates narrative's relation to fantasy as an attempt to belie the anxiety inherent in the search for the object. Castration is the sacrifice of jouissance; fantasy is the paradoxical enjoyment of that sacrifice. And so we keep writing.

But the Mainz Jews killed themselves. And the language of the Chronicle is quite clear in its insistence that we understand the deaths both as unprecedented acts and as acts comparable to the sacrifice of Isaac. So, should we read the homicides and suicides as the actual presentation of the potential sacrifice instigated through Isaac? Probably not. The Binding myth is to be read as if Isaac actually will have been sacrificed and, in an identical move, the weight of the Mainz offering is deferred: "May the blood of His devoted ones stand us in good stead and be an atonement for us and our posterity after us . . . like the *'Akedah* of our Father Isaac when our Father Abraham bound him upon the altar" (Eidelberg 49). Again, the events of the Chronicle are offered as comparable to the Binding, but with the understanding always implicit that this offering in every way exceeds the previous one.

So our question remains: How might we understand the narrative as a fantasy of completeness? In other words, what job does the Chronicle perform other than relating real events, even if the relation itself must by definition be a fiction? Here again we will turn to Žižek:

> Even when…God pronounces a concrete demand (ordering Abraham to slaughter his own son), it remains quite open what he really wants with it: to say that with this horrible act Abraham must attest to his infinite trust and devotion to God is already an inadmissible simplification. The basic position of

a Jewish believer is, then, that of Job: not so much lamentation as incomprehension, perplexity, even horror at what the Other (God) wants with the series of calamities that are being inflicted upon him. (*Sublime* 115)

Žižek's invoking of Job is not accidental. Both the Binding of Isaac and the Chronicle reference Job directly as antecedent to their respective narratives. In the Binding myth, Rashi offers one interpretation of the opening phrase (After these words . . .) as:

> after the words of Satan, who was accusing Abraham, and saying, "Out of the entire banquet that Abraham made, he did not offer before You one bull or one ram." God said to him, "Did he make the banquet for any reason at all other than for his son? If I were to say to him, 'Sacrifice him before me,' he would not refrain from doing it." [70] (Commentary to 22.1, 230)

The Chronicle's use of Job is less obvious, but other than the numerous explanations of the situation as a trial from God, there is at least one direct reference toward the beginning of the narrative, as Ivan Marcus points out, where the chronicler calls the Pope "'Satan,' the 'Accuser' in the Book of Job who challenges God to subject the righteous man to a supreme trial" (47). In this sense we might look to Job, not Abraham, as the founding father of the Jewish people, since it is Job who illustrates what it truly means to be chosen by God.

Regardless, Žižek's formulation of the desire of the Other as the desire of God is evocative. We should remember our understanding of the relation between Christians and Jews earlier in precisely these terms. The Binding myth reproduces nothing other than Abraham's (in)action when faced with the desire of God. And what Žižek calls "incomprehension, perplexity, even horror" is obvious in Rashi's commentary to 22.12, where Abraham questions God about His inconsistencies (235-236). The point is that there is no apparent object of God's desire other than the one offered by Rashi as a possible resolution in some future time. In the Chronicle, just as (or because of the fact that) the political situation shifts, so does the relation of the Jews of Mainz to their God. Homicide and suicide are presented not as the desire of God, but as demand: "all knew that this was a decree from God" (Eidelberg 28). And the object of God's demand seems to be the same as the Crusaders' demand: the very suffering inherent to what it means to be Jewish.

That the conflation of God's and the Crusaders' demand is necessary (and logical) should now be evident. The impulse toward narrative may be as simple as a move to address the commonplace "Why do bad things happen to good people?" The answer proposed is anything but commonplace. These "good people" become the chosen people in as much as the narrative sustains a reality in which the Crusaders and God may be separate(d). This explains the apparently contradictory polemic against Christians and the assumed justice of God. Though both have made a demand, God's demand understood in terms of the deferred desire of the Binding narrative forecloses the forced choice pushed by the Crusaders. But, at its essence, this fantasy also instigates its own lack. In order to reconcile the obscene demand of God's will toward jouissance with the promise that they are the chosen people, that God loves them, the Chronicle appeals (as it must through the very terms of this demand) to the founding narrative of the Binding of Isaac, thus reflexively constructing a fantasy of completeness. But the Binding myth itself is a narrative indicating its own lack in terms of its appeal to the future, that which we have marked as the logic of the future anterior. So the Chronicle, in its projection of a fantasy of completeness, must also assume this latter lack, and what we recognize as the *act* of the Chronicle as narrative is a peculiar traversing of fantasy: the exchange of a fantasy based on obscene jouissance, on demand, for a fantasy bound to the metonymic desire of the Other as God.[71]

In terms of trauma, we might recognize that the mass killing is not, strictly speaking, traumatic. The trauma *as it is marked by the narrative* is implicit in the obvious and constant search for precedent, in the gap between the two demands to which the participants responded, and in the insistence on the repetition of sacrifice as foundational for the people. The very fact that a cause is missing is enough reason to keep at making one.

Following our previous discussion of sacrifice and nonsacrifice, the Chronicle clearly offers a sacrificial understanding in as much as it does not posit (as both Girard and Kristeva do) some extrinsic or extratemporal support for the people but maintains that people through action, participation, now. That is, if the Christic innovation is to reveal that "the old sacrificial solutions are now bankrupt and completely empty" and seeks to end the victimage process, it may also foreclose the possibility of a kind of writing (Girard 241). There is a difference between constantly referring to a positive, logical, "true" cause like the Passion, God, the Mover, or Love and making an appeal that locates its utterer in history as an agent. Put another way, the metonymic rivalry illustrated by the Chronicle is between Crusader and God. The Chronicler's innovation is in assigning agency to the object and so allowing it (the people) to remove itself from the conflict. It is almost as if neither the good mother nor the bad mother would give up her claim and the child itself chooses the sword so that the good mother would not have to.

Regarding this fantasy of completeness, though, the jouissance-aspect of interpretation cannot be stressed too much. Narratives do have an effect. There is a very real sense in which the writing out of a testament or chronicle or poem provides a release from suffering in the same way that counseling or prayer might. What the above discussion indicates is that this relief has a great deal to do with the fantasy of completeness and that the jouissance here is better rendered by Lacan as joui-sense, that is, enjoying meaning. We should also admit here that much of what academic discourse involves falls under the heading of this brand of enjoyment. And, while there is nothing inherently wrong with enjoying one's work, it does seem that there should be something questionable about enjoying chronicles of other people's pain. The question, then, is how might one better approach these records, respect the truth of them, without falling into the trap of the fantasy of completeness or enjoying them too much, thus becoming the academic equivalent of Civil War reenactors.

5 What Stops Not Being Written

> *Each clue that comes is supposed to have its own clarity, its fine chances for permanence. But then she wondered if the gemlike "clues" were only some kind of compensation. To make up for her having lost the direct, epileptic Word, the cry that might abolish the night.*
>
> —Thomas Pynchon

When we are our most honest, we recognize the priority of theory as a practice in academic work. Midrash works at the level of the rupture, and the best work in English departments does too. We might modify Lacan to say that "if *academic inquiry* takes the Book literally, it is not in order to make it the bearer of more or less patent intentions, but because of its signifying collusion taken in its materiality...to draw another statement from the text: nay, to imply in the text what it itself neglected" (Handelman 154). When we speak or write about writing, for instance, we are always addressing what has gone without saying, the *caput mortuum*.

As with Freudian dream analysis, etc., we do not pretend (if we are honest) that the results produced by our studies are identical with the original product or its production. As Colette Soler argues:

> You can interpret a novel or poem—i.e., make sense of it—but this sense has nothing to do with the creation of the work itself. This sense has no common measure with the work's existence, and an enigma remains on the side of the existence of the work of art. This would even be a possible definition of the work in relation to sense: it resists interpretation as much as it lends itself to interpretation.[72] (Soler 214)

We are momentarily puzzled, for instance, when asked the naïve undergraduate question "But did the author really mean that?"

Whether or not the author meant it, the text certainly did insofar as it has provoked this particular response *right now*. That our response takes place and addresses questions *right now* indicates its rhetorical dimension. This response qua interpretation is not simply an arbitrary choice among an infinite number, but a special, temporal, contingent address to the irreducible void the work both conjures and masks. As Sharon Crowley points out: "A preference for contingency does not entail tolerance for all possibilities.... Some ways of believing have constructive effects, and others are simply destructive. Whether these effects are good or bad, of course, depends" (Crowley 56). Of the *good or bad* in the public sphere, Slavoj Žižek (probably predictably) takes the extreme position that

> [t]he temptation to be avoided here is the old Leftist notion of "better for us to deal with the enemy who openly admits his (racist, homophobic . . .) bias than with the hypocritical attitude of publically denouncing what one secretly and actually endorses." This notion fatally underestimates the ideologico-political significance of keeping up *appearances*: and appearance is never "merely an appearance," it profoundly affects the *actual* sociosymbolic position of those concerned. If racist attitudes were to be rendered acceptable for the mainstream ideologico-political discourse, this would radically shift the balance of the entire ideological hegemony. . . . Today, in the face of the emergence of new racism and sexism, the strategy should be to *make such enunciations unutterable*, so that any one relying on them automatically disqualifies himself (like, in our universe, those who refer approvingly to Fascism). (*Plague* 26)

Certainly, Žižek is addressing the rhetorical dimension of politics. The difficulty is that, rhetorically, the effect of disqualifying *approving* utterances often has the effect of also discounting critique, as when a blogger who complains about fascist tendencies in our own government—or in certain quadrants of the American population— is decried because fascism is unthinkable here, in the US of A. Regardless, the importance of *appearance* above should not be overlooked, because this is precisely the *image* discussed in the first chapter and is the master signifier as it covers over what is constitutively missing.

I. Discourse and Writing

In 1964, Vladimir Nabokov said, "A creative writer must study carefully the works of his rivals, including the Almighty. He must possess the inborn capacity not only of recombining but of recreating the given world" (*Strong Opinions* 32). Nabokov may have been naïve. How might a writer—a person ostensibly bent on creating something we might call literary—change the given set of signifiers generally accepted as reality? Certainly, the physical bound papers and the ink impressed on them are insufficient, as is any trope on the pen and the sword. Nabokov seems to indicate something else. What in the words themselves, not as physical entities but rather as discursive structures, organizes our understandings and unique apprehensions of a world? It may be that within creative texts, certain discourse structures become obvious, mappable structures that demonstrate possible architectures. I have said *a world*, because, with such a system, the number of signs may calculate the number of worlds, which could be practically infinite.

If Lacan is right in saying that there is no pre-discursive reality, then we should likely look to discourse for means of describing and supporting *real life*. And there are kinds of discourse, so it is in those kinds that one might discover exactly what is at stake in language in its determining role.

Lacan supposes that grammar is "that aspect of language that is revealed only in writing" (*Encore* 44). The context for the claim is, of course, an explanation (a defense) of his use of the letter in what he calls a mathematical sense: i.e., his mathemes and graphs. The concern with the formal—formal anything—becomes apparent and approachable *only in terms* of the appearance of form. Chronicles, textbooks, poems, or math equations are perhaps more approachable forms of writing, dealing as they do with what we might call *common language*. Everyone can participate in reading them, and so they supply apt examples. However, by extension, one might assume other forms of "writing" that have little to do, at least superficially, with texts. The symptom, for instance, can be understood as writing on the body when it appears. And oral cultures, that presumably have no formal script, nonetheless have ritual, myth, and totem. See Levi-Strauss, for example, who seeks to script the previously unscripted under the belief that such organizations or forms can be read. A definition of writing might then be: *that which can be read*. That is, it can be read after it appears.

Thus, the discourses outlined by Lacan might constitute ways of reading (a hermeneutics) as much as—or maybe more than—positions from which one may write. They also offer an occasion for more fun with mathemes. What follows is a quick primer on some Lacanian discourse structures.

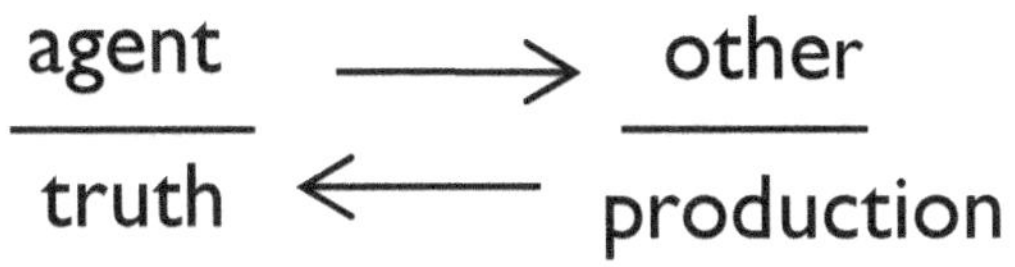

$$\frac{\text{agent}}{\text{truth}} \begin{array}{c} \longrightarrow \\ \longleftarrow \end{array} \frac{\text{other}}{\text{production}}$$

Figure 4. The Discourse Matheme.

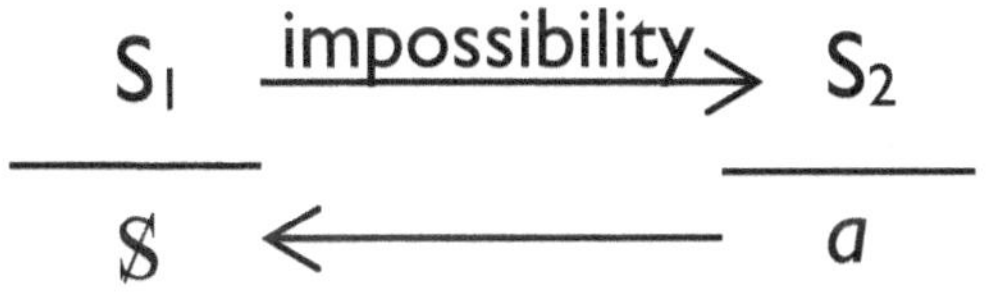

$$\frac{S_1}{\$} \begin{array}{c} \xrightarrow{\text{impossibility}} \\ \longleftarrow \end{array} \frac{S_2}{a}$$

Figure 5. The Discourse of the Master.

The master's discourse (Figure 5), also called the discourse of philosophy, assumes as the *agent* (a cause, a reason perhaps) a particular (master) signifier: S_1. From this predicate, one might then approach knowledge (S_2, the symbolic order) as meaning as an *other* to be investigated. It might help here to think of Plato's discussion of the soul and love in the Phaedrus. If one assumes the soul as primary to the individual (I am Mars-like fundamentally), one searches in the other for the same, for a likeness, from which one might find and found one's place in respect to that other; the master signifier here is a presumed essence and we should be able to find its likeness here in the physical realm. Note, however, that the move from the master signifier to the set of signifiers (as a body of knowledge) is marked as impossible because the assumption of the master signifier is really a presumption, the result of an earlier extrapolation taken as gospel. But according to Lacan, what is *produced* by this impossible relation (or this non-relating) is precisely the object-cause that is never reachable as such, but is rather the sign of the metonymy of desire (as discussed in the third chapter, this product may also be the abject as a remainder). The Other both promises a likeness and withholds it indefinitely. One might then define love as the recognition of the promise regardless of the fact that there is no sexual rapport. That is, love is precisely what makes up for that fact; the other's promise that I am loved balances the sheets. As Chaitin puts it, the philosopher "wants to find uniqueness by reproducing the 'identically identical' [the Mars-likeness], the pure particularity, of the original object of satisfaction [the supposed object-cause]" (9). The truth, then, of philosophical discourse is precisely the barred subject, the S/s (signifier/signified relation) with a new emphasis on the bar itself (as the mark of castration, of a substantive lack that is recognized as something lost). Žižek might say that the master discourse is concerned with construction rather than interpretation, inasmuch as lack is implicated by "a knowledge [here, in and of the Other] that can never be subjectivized—that is, it can never be assumed by the subject as the truth about himself" (*Plague*, Žižek 36). Knowledge is *out there* somewhere. Knowledge, however, should not be confused with *meaning* as the assumption of a positivized instance of the signifier (S_1) in its relation to the symbolic order (the S_2).

From this we might read the quarter turn that is the academic discourse (Figure 6) as an assumption of the knowledge that philosophy places extrinsic to itself (the realm of forms, say, or the works of Shakespeare). What was the product of philosophical inquiry is now the Other under investigation. For folks in English departments, this might be Shakespeare-as-category, that wholly supposed thing one might call Shakespeare-ness, a *je ne sais quoi* that even Francis Bacon might have. What is found, then, at the site of production is the barred-S that in our limited terms might here be figured as a critical edition of Hamlet, where competing readings are presented side by side, and the fact that they contradict might be read as the fact of the bar. Or one might say that, reading the barred-S as S/s, the signified "is not what you hear. What you hear is the signifier. The signified is the effect of the signifier" (Lacan 33). This effect—since a signifier is the subject for another signifier—is precisely the presentation of a master signifier as the truth of the academic discourse (rendered here in terms of impotence, since the master signifier is chosen to fill the hole made apparent by my inadequacy in finding the right Thing that will complete my relationship with the Other). Thus, I am ultimately able to declare that (in my investigations of Shakespeare) I am a Marxist and can present a Marxist reading of texts. Or even that I am a Lacanian.

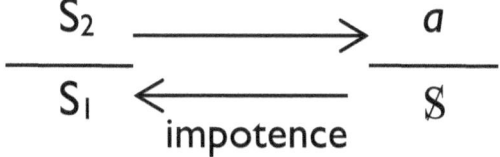

Figure 6. The Discourse of the Academy.

The analyst's discourse is difficult to illustrate in these sorts of terms precisely because it claims to be a way of reading—and, in fact, the way of establishing—the other discourses. That is, though I suggested that the discourses may be primarily ways of reading, it should be clear in the treatments above that they also illustrate modes of producing new texts. In fact, they may be the two primary modes. And, likely, any analyst bent on writing what he knows would work from these other two, since both assume knowledge as a priori (either as agent or other).

A difficulty with the two primary modes of discourse in the academy is their relationships to the master signifier. In the discourse of the master, the agent is the master signifier (that is another name for the phallic signifier in the fantasy of completeness). Thus, to work from the position of the master is to assume the agency of the phallus. The truth that supports this (mythic, narrative) signifier qua cause is the barred, cut, castrated subject of investigation and enjoyment (jouisense). Academic discourse, then, assumes the phallic function explicit in the master's as the ground for placing meaning in the position of agency. So, systematic meaning "is the ultimate authority" and the best bibliography wins (Fink 132).[73] Both discourses fall on the side of producing or supporting the fantasy of completeness that is bent on covering over, eliding, or effacing the fundamental paucity, even those marked by/as trauma. At best, working from these discourse (pre)dispositions increases the risks of totalizing (and killing) any utterance addressing trauma by excluding the excluded—the *caput mortuum*—from consideration.

Several years ago, a particularly bright undergraduate student of mine took up the notion of the *caput mortuum* nicely to write an essay dealing with the high school seasons (1997-1999) of the television program *Buffy the Vampire Slayer*. The argument was that Buffy Summers is the positive manifestation of what must be excluded from every clique or group in high school in order for those cliques or groups to exist. So, in order for there to be cheerleaders, Buffy must not be a cheerleader; in order for there to be a prom, she must miss it. Further, I would add that she offers a (mythic, narrative) resolution of adolescent social anxieties (anxieties being something like worries without objects) and the magical elements of the show are stand-ins for very complex problems that may have no simple real-life solutions. Thus, fraternity guys literally sacrifice high school girls to a giant snake and Buffy can behead the snake to end the fraternity and the phallic support of capital it also represents (companies headed by former members of the fraternity topple after the snake's head is lopped off). Again, narrative offers a resolution to what is irresolvable, at least so readily.

Fink's characterization of the *caput mortuum* is more complicated. His description depends upon the example of coin tosses. While at the level of each individual coin toss, the result is unpredictable; it can be heads or tails. But once tosses are catalogued and grouped together *after the fact*, the grouping reveals rules as to what could or could not have followed a heads or tails result (16-18). That is, once the tosses are *read*, a "restriction in terms of possibility has arisen, it seems, ex nihilo. Important too, though, is the *syntax* produced, that allows certain combinations and prohibits others" (19). This *after the fact* is important, since it is one way of saying that, at the level of (the coin-tossing) activity, rules are immanent and function much the same as the future anterior of the third chapter insofar as they will have been in effect. Fink claims that these rules postulate two separate levels of the Lacanian real: "(1) a real before the letter, that is, a pre-symbolic real, that, in the final analysis, is but our own hypothesis (R_1), and (2) a real after the letter that is characterized by impasses and impossibilities due to the relations among the elements of the symbolic order itself (R_2), that is, which is generated by the symbolic" (27). The pre-symbolic (pre-letter) real is precisely what Julia Kristeva is interested in when she investigates the pre-Oedipal situation, and the abject in Kristeva's formulation is a remainder very much like the *caput mortuum* as a mark of those impasses and impossibilities. As the *Oxford Essential Dictionary of Foreign Terms* situates our metaphor in terms of alchemy, the *caput mortuum* is "the residue remaining after distillation or sublimation."

The point here—and what makes the student's thesis above so interesting—is the translation of the positive and necessary cause discussed in the first chapter into something that is formally excluded and can only be apprehended by reading the structure afterwards (much like dream interpretation finds a cause that is never assumed to be *the* cause). Instead of a set being delimited by an outside, prior, and assumed force or cause, the chain of numbers (the symbolic order):

> Never ceases to *not* write the numbers that constitute the *caput mortuum* in certain positions, being condemned to ceaselessly write something else or say something which keeps avoiding this point, as though this point were the truth of everything the chain produces as it beats around the bush. One could go so far as to say that what, of necessity, remains outside the chain *causes* what is inside; something must, structurally speaking, be pushed outside for there to even be an inside. (27)

The *caput mortuum* is thus associated with that which is impossible in language and is a product of the symbolic order. In terms of this impossibility, and returning to the discussions of the first two chapters, we can re-characterize the *necessary* via Lacan as that which "doesn't stop being written" and the *contingent* as that which "stops not being written" (*Encore,* Lacan 94). I have described the Greco-Christian position in terms of the necessary, and would add that it maps nicely to the master's discourse. What this means is that the cause or agent of discourse (what can be said or written) is related to that which doesn't stop being written as the presumed exception that delimits the set, the master signifier qua phallus to which the set refers as a ground. Of course, what is produced in/by philosophic discourse is a remainder, a substance that does not quite fit the schema, an impossibility that nags in the way Paul's thorn in the flesh was said to, the symptom "characterized by impasses and impossibilities due to the relations among the elements of the symbolic order itself" (27).

The rabbinic, as I have portrayed it, takes up these impossibilities and plays them as far as they can be played in language. In effect, if the goal of midrash is "to draw another statement from the text: nay, to imply in the text what it itself neglected," that goal is precisely to stop not writing what the text qua myth is always already trying to cover over in the fantasy of completeness. Rabbinic (and, I argue, psychoanalytic) discourse seeks to clarify the fact of the impossible. One version of the impossible is, as we saw in the previous chapter, the impossibility of a sexual rapport. In terms of the second chapter's introduction of Lacanian sexuation, we can say that the reason sexual rapport is impossible is that the masculine and feminine positions are not at all complementary; the masculine speaks to fantasy as a way of covering over a substantive lack, and the feminine responds to the desire of the Other with indeterminacy because that lack is a fact.

II. History and Writing

So what does writing do to and for a notion of history, academic or otherwise? What happens to a supposed historical *event* in the writing of it? Jean Baudrillard writes that "[I]f there is something distinctive about...what constitutes an event and thus has historical value—it is the fact that it is irreversible, that there is always something in it which exceeds meaning and interpretation" (13). And writing (traditionally, at least) has been understood as a creature of meaning and interpretation. So what happens when meaning fails to capture an event? And, in such cases, what is the effect of writing as discourse as it both reveals its missing cause and tries to cover it up?

Any history that claims to be a simple statement of fact is, in essence, also doing something else. An essay entitled "What I Did on My Summer Vacation" may, in fact, discuss events that occurred in the three-month break, but the fact that these events are ordered and explained (and are given priority over all the others that occurred, too) indicates something over and above the simple statement "this happened." Such is likely obvious, but we need to stress it, since this understanding is what allows Caruth to read Freud's personal history (his moving from Germany to England, etc.) *with* the story he makes of/for Moses (Caruth 15, 17, 101). History isn't only an operation of metaphoric substitution, but has something to do with metonymy, as well. In other words, history has something to do with desire.

This is also Kenneth Burke's point in his discussion of motive and Kierkegaard, whose psychologizing of the Abraham story only makes sense in terms of his understanding of (and excuses for) his own behavior towards Regina. Kierkegaard is not amplifying some strand already in the text, but making a purely personal addition that makes best sense only in terms of the grammar (as the formal or relational structure loosely defined above) of his inscription. And it is this kind of meta-grammar that makes the sort of narrative we are taking about.

Perhaps we can approach this in another way, in terms of the hysteric's discourse (Figure 7). In the position of agent we have the a priori barred-S (another definition of which is the subject of the unconscious). The hysteric fundamentally recognizes a lack (the bar, the absence of a stable relation to a signified), that she then tries to cover with a master signifier available in and from some other (another person, an organization, "the poems of Sylvia Plath are about me!"). This then yields or produces a particular body of knowledge. The inadequate truth, though, posited by the hysteric is nothing other than the metonymy of desire. Thus, when Kristeva discusses the pre-symbolic in terms of the connection between mother and child, and the child's entrance into the symbolic as a violent separation from its mother (Kristeva 10), we might recognize Burke's astute observation that Kierkegaard uses another story besides the Abraham in the same discussion, that of the mother blackening her breast to make it unappealing. And this weaning, this loss, indicates the hysteric's position nicely as a "forever getting…by forever not getting," that I am relating to narrative (Burke 191).[74] Fundamental, formative trauma is only apparent in its *return*.

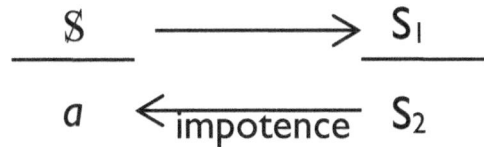

Figure 7. The Discourse of the Hysteric.

The writing (or the written-ness) of trauma narratives indicates that the trauma language circumscribes is not the event, but what the event "will have been," as that which marks the insufficiency of jouissance (the hysteric's discourse). Lacanian analysis reveals that history qua the story of trauma is that which is waiting for its cause. History in such a scheme is knowledge (S_2) as the product of an encounter with the positive version of the event after-the-fact (S_1). This knowledge is insufficient for the truth of the hysteric's discourse as the traumatic thing that is more than the single event: the object-cause.

So, what about narrative? In one sense, the truth of narrative isn't in the fact-checking, but in the trauma it circles. Lyotard assigns this motive to postmodern art and suggests such work "puts forward the un-presentable in presentation itself" (Lyotard 81). I would like to suggest that the presentation of the un-presentable is not so much in the work as it is in its reading, but the point is that narrative generally (even the Summer Vacation kind) indicates (or, rather, maybe produces an occasion for) a lack, and that perhaps those works we call art (literature and the rest) best drive that lack home.

As an example of the sort of work Lyotard is describing, and that I am arguing, proffers the object cause as its truth, consider Brian Eno's 1998 installation *Music for Prague*. Several years ago, I used this piece as an example of what I was calling the Postmodern Church,[75] and here I would like to modify my claims a bit.

Done in collaboration with Czech artist Jiri Prihoda, the installation consisted of temporary walls suspended from the ceiling inside the gallery space to enclose most of the room, with the framework of these walls faced towards the existing walls and with a gap maintained between the floor and the bottoms of the temporary walls. Visitors were left a hallway and benches around the enclosed area. Music was provided by twelve CD players visibly affixed to the temporary walls, all set to shuffle and randomly repeat the same piece of ambient music. Light came only from within the enclosed area (there was no way to enter it), where the light from outside the building came through the transparent ceiling and was reflected off of the floor and under the panels (Menotti).

The argument of this work seems to be Lyotard's, that post-modern art offers a frame for the un-presentable. In my previous exploration of the installation, I asked: "What is such an enclosed space—a space we cannot gain access to—but a physical manifestation of the infinite? That is, given that the music and play of light and color are (at least formally) eternal, isn't such a construct a way of giving the infinite body (matter) we can experience, if only temporarily?" (Richardson 225). Answering this question now, in the terms developed over the last few pages, I would say (invoking Victor Vitanza here) nes/yo (Vitanza 340). If we were to maintain a rigid notion of the forms, then there is perhaps a complete, idealized form of *Music for Prague* that was addressed at every moment in the changing work. This is to say that every experience of the installation was an incomplete experience and was thus presenting the signifier for completion (the master signifier) as an agent or cause in absentia (hence, the barred subject is the truth that supports the master signifier in the discourse of the master). On the other hand, if we imagine such art does not address the missing cause as a positivized, but deferred object (as a conflation of efficient and final cause that is then treated as if it were the formal cause), but is a presentation of the truth of that absence qua inadequacy of the fantasy of completeness (the impossibility of closing the set of all possible experiences), then the work is an Other that demands something from its viewers: attention, or at least their presence.[76]

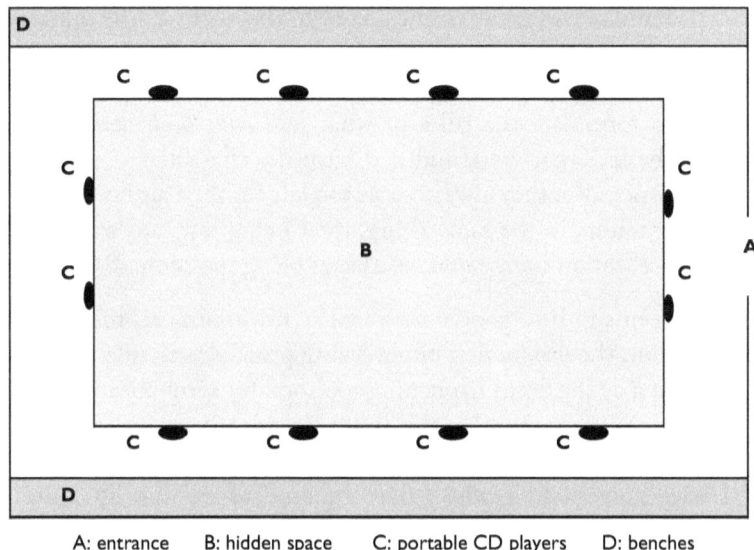

Figure 8. An approximation of *Music for Prague*. Illustration by the author.

The installation is generative (it cannot, by definition, repeat itself) but not arbitrary. It is certainly a *made* thing, but every experience of it is unique, that is, purely contingent as it addresses the present without a past or future. Since the work is always different, even for its makers, this example also makes Longinus' position that the author is aligned with the audience explicit so that, regarding another equally generative piece of his, the painting-generating software *77 Million Paintings* (Eno),[77] Eno maintains: "My experience of the piece is as fresh as the audience's. When I walk away from this tomorrow it'll carry on generating paintings—none of which I'll ever see—so every member of the audience will see a different set of images" (Eno and Carter). Such a situation has practical concerns, of course, since anyone could conceivably take an image from the software or a section of generative music and use it without the author's permission and the author would be hard pressed to prove it was his, since he has likely never seen or heard it before. Regardless, we might then assume Lyotard's position that:

> [a] postmodern writer or artist is in the position of a philosopher: the text he writes, the work he produces are not in principle governed by preestablished rules, and they cannot be judged according to a determining judgment, by applying familiar categories to the text or to the work. Those rules and categories are what the work of art itself is looking for. The artist and the writer, then, are working without rules in order to formulate the rules of what *will have been done*. Hence the fact that work and text have the characters of an *event*; hence also, they always come too late for their author, or, what amounts to the same thing, their being put into work, their realization (*mise en ouvre*) always being too soon. (81)

This seems to be a good assessment of my argument, too (the future anterior, the production of governing principles or rules after the fact, trauma as the event happening too soon for symbolization, etc.), with the small exception that this is precisely *not* the philosopher's position, at least as he is classically understood.

I have suggested elsewhere that the kind of art that literature is might be best considered in terms of the feminine (Richardson 96). This is perhaps another way of suggesting that the basic discourse of art/literature resembles that of the hysteric. Or, as Chaitin puts it, "a literary text may trace the contours of those gaps [the unpresentable, the substantive lack in the symbolic, the real] and bring out the places of singularity in which the subject may live" (9). In the field of desire, one lacks the signifier for completeness. The breast was blackened, etc. But of course the blackened breast itself is a placeholder, a signifier, for the formative event that cannot be written but is always being written about (*about* also in the sense of circumscribed—this is why people want to be writers, why people write diaries, and why everyone is writing a novel or screenplay), for what Caruth calls history as trauma. What must be stressed at this point is that the lack in question, at least after one's investment in the symbolic, is wholly sustained by the symbolic itself as a missing (exiled) cause that is formal in nature. The point may be simply that the metonymy of desire (the X_1- X_1- X_1 that doesn't find its X, its *a* or cause) is what supports the jouissance of writing, speaking, or believing, and that studying these (and writing about them), to be ethical, must take this jouissance into account.

One of the lessons of the story of the rabbis versus R. Eliezer in Chapter Two is that God, too, can offer interpretations of Torah. As an interpreter, we find God taking the same place as the author described in the first chapter, as colluding with the audience in his/their relation to the text.[78] The result is that the supposed author (God) and the audience are on the same side in regards to the Other qua text qua *that which can be read*. And we have discussed *text* as the Oral and Written Torah, but also as the kind of history Freud's *Moses and Monotheism* is when it is read the way Caruth does (in terms of the authorial history included in it), and as a trauma narrative that circumscribes the formative trauma that cannot itself be written. The point is that there is something that can never be accounted for in/by the text, and that something is now linked to the object *a* as the cause of desire and as that final cause that eludes apprehension because it is purely hypothetical and is in a manner of speaking a product of the text itself. That is, the cause is *supposed*, it *will have been*, and is not a priori.

On the side of the necessary—on which I have generally placed the classically Greek and Christian—we find the relationship of the subject with the Other is really one of fantasy, such that $\$ \Diamond a$ (or, at its most extreme, $\$ \Diamond \Phi$), and the Christian project is one of loving God by loving (what is missing from) oneself. As Lacan has it:

> But if before us God is dead, it is because he always has been dead, and that's what Freud says. He has never been the father except in the mythology of the son, or, in other words, in that commandment which commands that he, the father, be loved, and in the drama of the passion which reveals that there is resurrection after death. That is to say, the man who made incarnate the death of God still exists. He still exists with the commandment which orders him to love God. (*Ethics* 177)

Without plowing through Lacan's long discussion in seventh seminar[79] regarding the death of God as the myth for the foundation of the Law, consider the following: the Christian paradox is that, just as the introduction of the son both assumes and creates a father, communion with the son (being Christ-like, as Christ as the *logos ensarkos* made incarnate God's death) makes the father as an active player irrelevant; God becomes a formal cause (like food lying west), the signifier for what we (men) by definition lack. We should, as good Christians, love God precisely because to love God as Father is to recognize our own inadequacy (castration) reflected back from beyond as a promise of (eventual) wholeness. Put another way: "As a specular mirage, love is essentially deception. It is situated in the field established at the level of the pleasure reference, of the sole signifier necessary to introduce a perspective centered (sic) on the Ideal point, capital I, placed somewhere in the Other, from which the Other sees me, in the form I like to be seen" (*Four Fundamental Concepts* 268). Such is, after all, Platonic love in a nutshell.

If my project is rhetoric as an atheism of sorts (as I suggested in Chapter Two), then we should probably translate the death of God in any case into something else, something that has more to do with the production of cause after the fact. In *The Four Fundamental Concepts of Psycho-Analysis*, Lacan makes the claim that "the true formula of atheism is not *God is dead*—even by basing the origin of the function of the father upon his murder, Freud protects the father—the true formula of atheism is *God is unconscious*" (*Four Fundamental Concepts* 59). If we read this with the position Lacan takes throughout his teaching, that the unconscious is the discourse of the Other, then do we arrive at a point where we can say that God is the *discourse* of the Other? Perhaps. The function of God in such a scheme would be as the stand-in for what cannot be symbolized except as an exception, as what is always being talked about as the condition of/for jouissance— the object cause of desire, object *a*—that is, as we saw Žižek explain in the previous chapter, an object produced by the very metonymy defining desire. So, when Lacan says that man's desire is always desire of the Other, and if God is not the Other, then God is the Other's desire? Again, perhaps. Men desire something from the Other, and that something is what the Other desires, only this last desire is presented as a demand (love me). And if God is dead, it is because "[o]bject *a* is no being. Object *a* is the void presupposed by a demand, and it is only by situating demand via metonymy, that is, by pure continuity assured from the beginning to the end of a sentence, that we can imagine a desire that is based on no being" (*Encore* 126). Perhaps, for those on the masculine side of sexuation, God is the *bar* since "the function of the bar is not unrelated to the phallus" (39). We discussed God's demand in its relation to desire in the previous chapter. Here, however, we have a new formulation of God as the signifier for what is lacking *and* as the demand that orders one to give the lack up (and enjoy it).

If I have said that, for the rabbis, God is missing, it is only because—much as the author participates with his audience in Longinus—God is assumed to their side in relationship with the Other as text. Accordingly, the rabbis find themselves in a very different association with the Other, S(A̶), and take their place as the object of the Other's desire. The rabbis assume their own cause imminently, contingently, and have no need for a formal and extrinsic cause as Aristotle and Augustine would posit.

By positioning rhetoric on the side of contingency, I am maintaining that in some sense the God of Rhetoric is absent as an extrinsic cause, or perhaps it is the cause that must be elided in order for there to be something to talk about (hence, the Buffy of Rhetoric). That is, for the rhetorician, the object of study is the ruptures in saying, in whatever is not being *said* in whatever saying is being investigated. Lacan states: "It is at the very point at which paradoxes spring up regarding everything that manages to be formulated as the effect of writing that being presents itself, always presents itself, by para-being" (*Encore* 45). By *para-being*, Lacan means to posit that, "language imposes being upon us and obliges us, as such, to admit that we never have anything by way of being" (44). Essentially, language imposes subject-hood upon us, but from very close by. Fink argues that the excluded signifier that would pin down identity (and being itself) is excluded *on the inside* such that "it is what is most intimate, but at the same time ejected out of oneself, hence extimate; it is thus exterior while remaining terribly intimate, and interior while remaining utterly foreign" (Fink 183n). Isn't this much like Eno's installation described above? Ultimately, then, against the notion of the extrinsic to which I have attached the Greco-Christian philosophical/religious project, we would offer the psychoanalytic (/rabbinic/artistic/rhetorical?) notion of the extimate as that which is in me but foreign,[80] or as that part that is not-all. We may, as Plato did, feel the need to posit being as eternal (really, beyond time) so that my essence or soul is ultimately literally formal, but Lacan's point seems to be that, while such a position may seem necessary from a particular standpoint, cause need not be so very far away. Perhaps it is here right now.[81]

III. Contemporary History?

I have said almost nothing up to this point about contemporary rhetorical studies except to place them in humanities programs. To some extent, I have neglected the present because part of the *raison* for this project is to trouble the grounds on which (some) contemporary rhetoric has been built by supplying an additional historical (in the simple, vulgar sense) precedent that is both Western and resistant to the traditional Greco-Christian cannon: rabbinic thought and practice.

One need not necessarily look to rabbinic thought for some of these insights, of course. Early in her excellent *Toward a Civil Discourse: Rhetoric and Fundamentalism*, Sharon Crowley maintains that "[a] contemporary theory of rhetoric must do more than revive ancient notions, however; it must adapt old notions to address contemporary rhetorical situations" (47). Crowley follows this by reviewing the sophistic position on *doxa* (as *expectation* and as the term that "designates current and local beliefs that circulate communally"), and then follows by elaborating on Protagoras's *logoi*, worth quoting at some length:

> Contending *logoi* make the world apparent. Protagoras's notorious "man-measure" doctrine makes sense in the context of his epistemology of clashing opposites: human beings perceive and select from among the available multitude of contending *logoi* those that address a particular moment and location. Humans are indeed the "measure" of all things, because it is they who perceive, evaluate, choose, and express from among the plentitude of *logoi* thrown off by things in the world.... Janet Atwill argues that because of the plentitude of available *logoi*, Protagoras's "doctrine maintained that subjectivity is contingent on incalculable specificities, encompassing physical perception itself. The dictum challenged static models of both subjectivity and 'reality'" (19).
>
> In other words, subjectivities, and our impressions of reality itself, are mobile, various, and contingent on circumstance. The *logoi* that get taken up are also temporal, local, and contingent, although thanks to language (and to writing in particular), upon their articulation humans may begin to treat them as though they continually refer to some stable reality. That is, their rhetoricity, their performativity, can easily be overlooked or forgotten. (48)

Protagoras's position as described above works nicely with our characterization of rabbinic accounts, especially when compared to Susan Handelman's description of the Hebrew *davar* as a word-thing:

> Names are not conventional, but intrinsically connected to their referents; the name, indeed, is the referent for the thing, its essential character—not the reverse, as in Greek thought. One does not pass beyond the name as an arbitrary sign towards a non verbal vision of the thing, but rather *from the thing to the word*, which creates, characterizes, and sustains it. Hence *davar* is not simply *thing* but also *action, efficacious fact, event, matter, process.* (32)

The *logoi* seem to do much the same work that *davar* does insofar as they are both invested in contingency, rhetoric as action and event, etc. Handelman's *Greeks* above are of course the classical philosophers who replaced Protagoras and who give us (master-signifier) Philosophy. What an appeal to Protagoras may not be able to do very well, however, is explain how the Greek position is taken up by Christianity and how this collusion affects our understanding of the written for a very long time.

As we have seen, the *logos ensarkos* becomes a very special instance of the word, and, afterwards, the Old Testament (much like a father, its name changes with the investment of a son) becomes the old words that prefigure the new Word, and the old words take on the status of signs. Susan Handelman describes the relationship thusly:

> The tendency to *gather* various meanings *into a one* is…characteristic of Greek thought in general: its movement towards the universal, the general, the univocal. The Rabbinic tendency, by contrast, is towards differentiation, metaphorical multiplicity, multiple meanings. One needs to search the forms, shapes, patters of words, and their varying meanings within the expansive text; there is no confinement of meaning within the ontology of substance. . . .
>
> Whereas for the Jews, God manifested Himself through words in a divine text, for the Greeks, theophany was visual, not verbal—a direct, immediate appearance of the gods. Thus, in the Hellenistic era, the divine logos ultimately became, through the influences of Neoplatonism, Stoicism, and Christianity—visible theophany. (33)

All of this is to say that, for Crowley's project, at least—as it is an investigation of Christian fundamentalisms in the United States—a more nuanced version of how certain positions were marked off early on might be useful.[82] As it is, Crowley's argument that the current tensions are between two hegemonies in public discourse—Enlightenment-style liberalism and Christian fundamentalism—is informative, useful, and often brilliant. But I would suggest that both of these hegemonies are, in fact, opposing points on the same mobius strip, which is to say that they come from a common (classical) father, and siblings often bicker.

Not coincidentally, Handelman invokes above the One in Greek thought. Lacan troubles the myth of the One (which is certainly related to the fantasy of completeness, courtly love, etc.) by positing that "there are two plus a. This two plus a, from the standpoint of a, can be reduced, not to the two others, but to a One plus a" (*Encore* 49). What Lacan is describing is the relationship $\$\lozenge a$, fantasy, where the two or more can be taken as One insofar as something is excluded. Thus, "[b]etween two, whatever they may be, there is always the One and the Other, the One and the a, and the Other cannot in any way be taken as a One" (49). Lacan describes this relation of ones as a ternary relationship, as two with something else between them, so instead of S/S, we have, say, S-O-S or S-a-S (or even M-O-M!), and the Other or the object should be considered extimate in the manner Fink describes. The result is that "[i]t is insofar as something brutal is played out in writing (*l'ecrit*)—namely, the taking as ones of as many ones as we like [as many S_1s as we like]—that the impasses that are revealed thereby are, by themselves, a possible means of access to being for us and a possible reduction of the function of that being in love" (49). So, writing (or language) both offers the possibility of access to being—as language imposes being on us, a being predicated on the impossibility of sexual rapport—and offers the possibility of making up for that impossibility in being with (ultimately impotent) love.

It is puzzling, then, that while Crowley finds something useful for her project in Lacan's work, she completely rejects formative lack—and so the barred subject ($\$$)—on which so much of Lacan's teaching rests. In a note to page 93, she writes:

> This aspect of Lacan's theory [apparently, the loss of the presymbolic Real] is troubling because it establishes a formidable black hole at the center of human being. It is hard to rational-

ize activism, or much of anything else, from lack as a starting point. Deleuze and Guattari take Lacan to task on this point in *Anti-Oedipus* (25-35). They argue that his introduction of this "Great Other" into his theories reinscribes it in the very modes of thought from which Lacan tried to escape. In the spirit of *bricolage* I put Lacan's thought to use while refusing to adopt his positioning of absolute absence at the heart of desire. (210)

I am resistant to this caveat for several reasons, the least important of which is that I don't think Deleuze and Guattari are really taking Lacan to task. They write: "Desire does not lack anything; it does not lack its object. It is, rather, the *subject* that is missing in desire, or desire that lacks a fixed subject; there is no fixed subject unless there is repression" (26). I would suggest reading this in terms of Lacan's discussion of the One above, where he suggests that "two plus a, from the standpoint of a, can be reduced, not to the two others, but to a One plus a" (*Encore* 49). That is, Deleuze and Guattari are speaking from the standpoint of a, where the fixed subject (a One) is possible only via the insertion of something else, repression (of trauma) as the mark of what returns. Admittedly, Lacan's description of the One and a is from 1974, two years after Deleuze and Guattari published *Anti-Oedipus* (so perhaps he learned from them), but we can find a similar position in *The Other Side of Psychoanalysis*, where Lacan argues:

> We can observe that historically the master has slowly defrauded the slave of his knowledge [S_2] and turned it into the master's knowledge. But what remains a mystery is how the desire to do this could have arisen for him. Desire, if you take my word on this, he can easily do without, since the slave satisfies him even before he himself knows what he might desire. (34)

Because man's desire is the Other's desire, that desire is positive (not lost) makes sense insofar as the master's is primarily a masculine discourse, since "in the simple functioning of the relations between the master and slave, it is clear that the master's desire is the Other's desire, since it's this desire that the slave anticipates" (38). Thus, from the master's position, desire is constituted retroactively by (is a product of) the slave's response (I desire cake because I was brought cake), and so the object isn't lost but is that which constitutes desire as a positive experience.[83] But what functions as desire for the master is often experienced as demand by the slave, and anticipating that demand is the jouissance of the slave.[84]

Perhaps the basic model of such an exchange is best illustrated by infancy, where, as Fink describes,

> One cannot even say that a child *knows* what it wants prior to the assimilation of language: when a baby cries, the *meaning* of that act is provided by the parents or caretakers who attempts to name the pain the child seems to be expressing (e.g., "she must be hungry"). There is perhaps a sort of general discomfort, coldness, or pain, but its meaning is imposed, as it were, by the way in which it is interpreted by the child's parents. If a parent responds to its baby's crying with food, the discomfort, coldness, or pain will retroactively be determined to have "meant" hunger, as hunger pangs. One cannot say that the true meaning behind the baby's crying was that it was cold, because meaning is an ulterior product: constantly responding to a baby's cries with food may transform all of its discomforts, coldness, and pain into hunger. Meaning in this situation is thus determined not by the baby but by other people, and on the basis of the language they speak. (6)

The object of desire might be said to be extimate inasmuch as causation is foisted on an Other and then returns as a positive object. I have offered the above as an example of a first master/slave relationship, that implies that our children are our masters. But we should also notice that this economy of return as a *meaning* (this is, how language imposes being on us) bears a marked resemblance to love as we have considered it. Thus, we may love our children, but perhaps it's the kind of love best called Stockholm syndrome.

With desire linked as it is to meaning, my reading of Deleuze and Guattari is that they propose another discourse to that of the master, and this is precisely the discourse Lacan proposes, too, in *The Other Side of Psychoanalysis*.[85] The analyst's discourse takes the position of agency as the object cause of desire (*Encore* 38). Where, in the hysteric's discourse the object cause was the truth supporting the subject, for the analyst the barred subject takes the place of the other in a relationship described as impossible (as the object as cause has yet to be constituted and is thereby only supposed—as in "the subject supposed to know"). What is produced by this discourse is a master signifier by which the analysand might found a place with respect to the Other, and the truth supporting the analyst in her position as cause is a knowledge that is presumed by the subject.

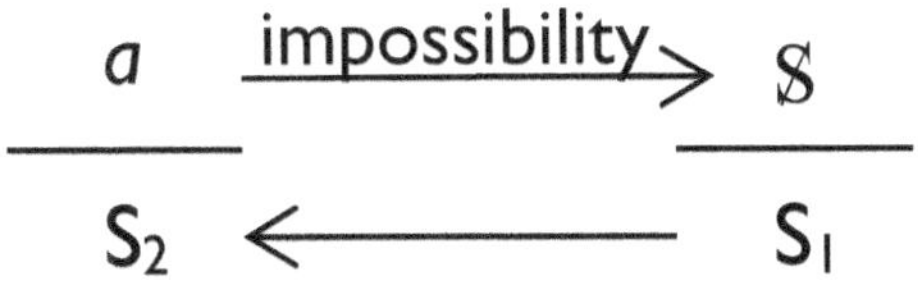

$$\frac{a \xrightarrow{\text{impossibility}} \$}{S_2 \longleftarrow S_1}$$

Figure 9. The Discourse of the Analyst.

The production of master signifiers is one reason Mark Bracher (whom Crowley cites) argues for a psychoanalytically informed writing pedagogy. He writes:

> The process of ego consolidation through promoting master signifiers[86] can thus involve more than just rehearsing one's prior knowledge and beliefs. It can also involve exploring and colonizing codes or experiences that have not yet been incorporated into our identity. In such cases our writing can alter our own identity-bearing master signifiers. And over time, the alteration can be substantial, as bits and pieces of formerly alien values, beliefs, and knowledge become integrated into our sense of identity and reality. (47)

Thus, Crowley is correct in arguing that "[p]eople who fantasize identity with whatever is depicted by one or more master signifiers" do so because they want recognition or love from the Other, and when someone (or a group of someones) does not want identity designated by the same signifier, the former "can become alienated and even enraged by this challenge to a fantasized communal identity" (95). Such is *doxa*. But it is also true that master signifiers can change, and *activism* is precisely the activity of seeking to change these signifiers. The institution of the bar for the subject (the fact that the subject is not identical with itself) is what opens up a space for these signifiers to take root.[87]

In a certain sense, though, these master signifiers are really the positive forms of the object cause after it has returned from the Other. They are products that arise from either belief in or faith in the Other, as we saw in the second chapter. So, for a proper excavation of the object cause of desire as the telos of rhetoric (in my understanding, Burke calls the object cause *motive*), we should likely return to discussions of *a*. Crowley begins her psychoanalytically inspired section by stating "I have wondered how rhetoricians can do without a theory of desire" (92). Of course, I suggest we try Lacanian theory. And before leaving Crowley's book, we should notice that she, in fact, treats the Enlightenment/Fundamentalism divide in the same way that Lacan describes the One, so that between the Enlightenment and Christian Fundamentalist hegemonies she injects an Other in the form of rhetoric, and the possible *in(ter)ventions* she proposes are precisely the sort of extimate implications midrash and psychoanalysis are and rhetoric can be.

IV. THE OBJECT CAUSE AND MOTIVE

Staying briefly with discussions of fundamentalism and the substitution of signifiers, in his short essay "Axis Thinking," Brian Eno suggests:

> What characterizes fundamentalism is a set of extremely narrow axes that allow almost no movement, no experimentation. And liberalism is perhaps the attempt to keep the axes as open as possible without incurring complete social fragmentation. The importance of symbolic behaviors like art and religion and sexual fantasy is that they allow us to experiment symbolically with new and even prohibited positions on the axial matrix—experiments that may be inconvenient, dangerous and divisive in "real life." (302)

When I teach this essay, the phrase that students often find startling is "symbolic behaviors like art and religion and sexual fantasy." We have talked about all three, and this may be what Charles Taylor means when he says that the move to secularity does not elide religion, but is at last an admission that there may be other options to religion (3). Eno's point (and mine) is that these behaviors are precisely *behaviors*, performances that are contingent upon one's position in the symbolic matrix. And these performances may be read after the fact (after their event) rhetorically as being addressed to a perceived lack in the symbolic (as experiments always address something missing) that is engendered and projected back, as it were, by the fact of their performance. That is, such experimentation—art, religion, sex, whatever—creates (an occasion for) its own cause.

To treat such experiments as rhetorical would be to treat them as both *products* and *instigations* of contingent, local, cultural, ultimately symbolic matrices that circle a cause that cannot be rendered intelligible otherwise. Like the black hole in Crowley's note, we know the cause is there because there is an effect. And, of course, what we call that cause after we read it has its own effects.

But what are these later effects?

Against individual *being*, Lacan posits ex-sistence as that which is propped up by the symbolic order. *Being*, he argues, "is merely presumed in certain words—'individual', for instance, and 'substance'. In my view, it is but a fact of what is said" (*Encore* 118). Said by whom? Or, rather, said by what? Lacan says:

> Analysis can be distinguished from everything that was produced by discourse prior to analysis by the fact that it enunciates the following, which is the very backbone of my teaching—I speak without knowing it. I speak with my body and I do so unbeknownst to myself. Thus I always say more than I know. (119)

Such is the analytic symptom as that which can be read. The symptom is a kind of flare-up of a symbolic impasse. Lacan continues:

> This is where I arrive at the meaning of the word "subject" in analytic discourse. What speaks without knowing it makes me "I," subject of the verb. That does not suffice to bring me into being. That has nothing to do with what I am forced to put into being—enough knowledge for it to hold up, but not one drop more. (119)

Thus, the subject as such has nothing to do with being, but is a position in the symbolic matrix that is "never more than fleeting and vanishing, for it is a subject only by a signifier to another signifier" (142). On what speaks—the body that speaks (for) the *I*—Lacan elaborates:

> This is what was hitherto called form. In Plato's work, form is the knowledge that fills being. Form doesn't know any more about it than it says. It is real in the sense that it holds being in its glass, but it is filled right to the brim. Form is the knowl-

edge of being. The discourse of being presumes that being is, and that is what holds it. (119)

Lacan gives the *discourse of being* a body, what he finds in Plato is form. This form is in one sense literally the body proper as something that speaks *about* what cannot be said as any knowledge, since this knowledge is precisely knowledge of the impossible (Lacan's master discourse demonstrates this impossibility) as that which doesn't stop being written. That is, what doesn't stop being written as a symptom on the body is an effect of discourse as a formal (and necessary) structure, which is taken as a cause after the fact, in much the same manner that narrative creates its object by the act of covering it up. Finally, then:

> There is some relationship that cannot be known. It is that relationship whose structure I investigate in my teaching, insofar as that knowledge—which, as I just said, is impossible—is prohibited thereby. This is where I play on an equivocation—that impossible knowledge is censored or forbidden, but it isn't if you write "inter-dit" appropriately—it is said between the words, between the lines. (119)

The psychoanalytic innovation is transmuting the classical, extrinsic cause into the extimate cause that is both engendered by formal (grammatical, etc., as with the coin tosses) and is supposed in the logic of *what will have been*. The impossible knowledge is precisely the possibility of a signifier for completion (Φ or S_1) that is the impossibility of sexual rapport.

What can be written—what stops not being written—is the impossibility itself: "The 'I' is not a being, but rather something attributed to [or presumed in] that which speaks. That which speaks deals only with solitude" and "[t]hat solitude, as a break in knowledge, not only can be written but it is that which is written *par excellence*, for it is that which leaves a trace of a break in being" (Lacan 120). That Lacan is maintaining a distinction between *saying* and what is *written* makes sense insofar as "[t]he signified is not what you hear. What you hear is the signifier. The signified is the effect of the signifier" (33). One does not hear what is meant in a saying, but rather one reads what has been said and interprets it by implying in it what has (necessarily) gone without saying. It is the reading of what has been written that is the project of psychoanalysis; this is, as we have seen, also the rabbinic project, since there are many things that can be read.

Here we find the common ground between psychoanalysis and the position of rhetoric I am advocating. What both consider and in some sense describe is discovered via (and is constituted by) the structure of the written and is not in the intended *meaning* ("what the author really meant") of whatever text is the focus of analysis. Lacan argues:

> For every speaking being, the cause of its desire is, in terms of structure, strictly equivalent, so to speak, to its bending, that is, to what I have called its division as subject [$]. That is what explains why the subject could believe for so long that the world knew as much about things as he did. The world is symmetrical to the subject—the world of what I . . . called thought is the equivalent, the mirror image, of thought. (127)

That is, "the world of being, full of knowledge, is but a dream, a dream of the body insofar as it speaks, for there is no such thing as a knowing subject," so that the world is not pre-given but a projection outward of the cause of desire and a bending—much like a funhouse mirror or the famous anamorphic distortion— such that that object is positivized as a supposed knowledge *somewhere else* (126). Thus, Lacan claims:

> This mirror is what allowed for the chain of beings that presupposed in one being, said to be the Supreme Being, the good of all beings. Which is also the equivalent of the following, that object *a* can be said to be, as its name indicates, *a*-sexual. The Other presents itself to the subject only in an *a*-sexual form. Everything that has been the prop, the substitute prop [S_1, etc.] or substitute for the Other in the form of the object of desire is *a*-sexual. (127)

Here we find what allows Brian Eno to place art, religion, and sexual fantasy in the same company. We have already discussed in what manner art (as something that can be read) addresses its missing cause. We can talk about religion and sexual fantasy in the same manner insofar as both are ways of covering over—often via narrative—the fundamental antagonism Žižek describes, that is always a surfacing, so to speak, of the object cause of desire. Thus, with Lacan's *a*-sexual we can propose the *a*-theological. In terms of religion, the Other as the supposed First Person is the theological substitute for the object-cause produced or summoned by religion's own narrative. So, in the religious dimension, traversing fantasy would be the move from theology to *a*-

theology, from belief in the One to faith in the Other. What we find is the replacement of an extrinsic Law with a practice that takes as its cause the extimate implicated by performance.

I have argued for a rhetoric that begins from the discourse of analysis as a way of describing a move away from philosophy, since rhetoric has historically been linked to the philosophical project, and I have characterized this difference as an insistence on contingency over the necessary. If we return (finally) to discussions of love, Lacan states:

> I incarnated contingency in the expression "stops not being written." For there is nothing but encounter, the encounter in the partner of symptoms and affects, of everything that marks in each of us the trace of his exile—not as subject but as speaking—his exile from the sexual relationship. Isn't that tantamount to saying that it is owing to the affect that results from this gap that something is encountered, which can vary infinitely as to the level of knowledge, but which momentarily gives us the illusion that the sexual relationship stops not being written?—an illusion that something is not only articulated but inscribed, inscribed in each of our destinies, by which, for a while—a time during which things are suspended—what would constitute the sexual relationship finds its trace and its mirage-like path in the being who speaks. The displacement of the negation from the "stops not being written" to the "doesn't stop being written," in other words, from contingency to necessity—there lies the point of suspension to which all love is attached. All love, subsisting only on the basis of the "stops not being written," tends to make the negation shift to the "doesn't stop being written," doesn't stop, won't stop. (145)

Love, then, facilitates the move from the contingent to the necessary. That is, love makes it possible to assume a formal cause from the evidence of the material and efficient, that is then often confused or collapsed with the final cause. If the rhetorical is going to (re)discover the contingent nature of its subject, it can only do so by turning back from the philosophical, by becoming its mirror image, by taking the place of the cause for its subject in order to imply in the subject what the subject cannot say, but nonetheless performs daily.

Notes

1. For possible answers, see *The Gift, Bend Sinister, Pnin, Ada, Transparent Things, Look at the Harlequins*, and any number of other sources. See also Brian Boyd, *Nabokov's Ada: The Place of Consciousness* (245).

2. One reason no archival footage was used in Claude Lanzmann's *Shoah* would seem to be that anything archival would invoke a feeling that, as history, the events were inevitable. The genius of solely relying on accounts is that the events described seem *present* in the bodies of the speakers.

3. See Thomas Stearns Eliot, "Tradition and the Individual Talent" and Harold Bloom, *The Anxiety of Influence: A Theory of Poetry*, 2nd ed. (157), respectively.

4. See Aristotle for this kind of hierarchy: "Words spoken are symbols or signs of affections or impressions of the soul; written words are the signs of words spoken" (Aristotle and Cooke 115).

5. Consider, too, Sergey Dolgopolski's "What is the Sophist? Who is the Rabbi?" for Classical approaches to rabbinic hermeneutics (Hughes and Wolfson 253; Dolgopolski 333).

6. See Nathan Widder, "What's Lacking in the Lack: A Comment on the Virtual" (117).

7. Much of my understanding of Deleuze's position on lack and my final example here depend heavily on conversations with Levi Bryant, whose excellent book on Deleuze (Levi R. Bryant, *Difference and Givenness : Deleuze's Transcendental Empiricism and the Ontology of Immanence* is highly recommended.)

8. Thus, the polymorphously perverse body is carved into erogenous zones.

9. In this discussion, Plato goes through a process of division ending with proportional relations. Here, following Kennedy (*Classical Rhetoric* 50), we should point out simply that these proportions (gymnastics, medicine, etc.) have a temporal relation in that the first member of each pair is normative and looks toward the future, while the second is corrective and has to do with setting right the wrongs of the past (one does gymnastics to affect one's future health and appeals to medicine to address one's lack of gymnastics when young).

10. Yousef Z. Liebersohn argues that, at the time of the composition of *Gorgias*, rhetoric was "rising." Rhetoric was "still in formation" and "[t]he only person who can cope with this intermediate stage is the philosopher. An ordinary person sees with his eyes, but the philosopher sees also with his mind's eye. We could say that the philosopher is a sort of prophet. He is capable of looking at something which is still taking shape and identifying its nature and essence" (Liebersohn 38). This is not a position I am willing to agree with, of course, but most interesting here for our purposes is the evocation of prophecy as a characteristic of philosophy (if only via simile).

11. At the same time, "*empirical* personality can be looked upon as sharing in the spirit of the *supernatural* personality" (*Religion* 38). The Christian innovation is positing Christ as whole, as the literal embodiment of love qua logos. For Christ as logos, see the later discussion of Augustine in this chapter; for Christ as logos/love, see the third chapter.

12. Mathew S. Linck makes the point that, in *Phaedrus*, "[o]nce the path of *eros* as the subject of discourse has been established, a certain circumlocution is necessary.... It is a circuitous and quasi-dissembled leading that speaks a partial truth about something one could never speak about without resorting to saying 'what it is like'" (Linck). If we can say that the simile is a kind of likeness, Linck's point that the dialogue performs its topic rather than says it works well with the discussion of appearance here and below.

13. Here we have the misrecognition of lack as loss, the structuring function of lack as *manque-à-être*; see Jacques Lacan, *The Four Fundamental Concepts of Psycho-Analysis* (29).

14. We might then assume that the recognition of different audiences is the purview of philosophy, whereas the consideration of them as one expounds or discusses is rhetorical.

15. Kennedy's translation of the above passage is perhaps better in some regards for our discussion. His uses the more scientific genus-species categories rather that the gloss "kinds," for instance, and differs from the passage as quoted in that, whereas the former has "within human limits," Kennedy renders it "in so far as the nature of speech is capable," laying the weight of inadequacy squarely on the shoulders of language. Apparently, human beings can contemplate without speaking (59).

16. We might assume, for instance, that a novel, story, or poem points toward something external to the plot. Thus, the kind of historicism that claims that a novel must say something about its temporal/cultural location also claims that there is a logical relationship between the literary work and some assumed principle—say, sexual identity—and that the literary work is a contemporary answer to a timeless question. We need only discover the premise implicit in this conclusion (this novel). Of course, one counter to such claims is that the issue at hand is really the critic's issue and the literary work is useful to illustrate the issue or question itself. But, then, the assumption is

that these are universal principles after all, so whether or not the author or the critic brings them to the table may be beside the point. More charitably (and more honestly) one might allow that the use of the novel in the development of some theory of sexuality is a *rhetorical* use insofar as it is mostly invested in how the work (however old) does something for us *right now*.

17. George Kennedy suggests in a note to Aristotle's positing rhetoric as a counterpart to dialectic that Aristotle "does not entertain the possibility that dialectic should be regarded as a species of rhetoric, perhaps because dialectic appeals to universals, rhetoric with specifics; dialectic is logically prior": See Aristotle and George Alexander Kennedy, *On Rhetoric: A Theory of Civic Discourse* (39n). Here we find the logical prior associated with universals and the secondary attached to specifics. Might it be possible to read the Father/Son relationship discussed next in these terms, too, so that the Son is treated in terms of specifics (and the Passion is thus somehow a rhetorical act)?

18. Burke makes this point explicit in *The Rhetoric of Religion: Studies in Logology* (218).

19. We can also see the Passion functioning as both final cause (an end, as it sets in motion the Second Coming) and as efficient cause, since the Christ is in us (*Rhetoric of Religion*, Burke 254).

20. One reading of Graham Harmon's *Prince of Networks* is as an attempt to extend persuasion to things: "[N]ever forget that 'those being talked to' and 'those being convinced' include inanimate objects. A charlatan might convince a roomful of dupes that they can walk on hot coals without being harmed, but the coals remain unconvinced—leading the charlatan into lawsuits or beatings from his angry mob of victims" (Harman 23). What has to go ignored in this analogy is that the charlatan has already been named as such; his clients are dupes and victims before they walk, and apparently the coals are unconvinced because they already know.

21. Charles Taylor makes a similar point when he argues that secularity is the acknowledgement that there are other options to the religious—see Charles Taylor, *A Secular Age* (3). As broad-minded as this position is, my point is that this is not what we usually mean by *secular* in the academy; secularity is almost always aligned against religiosity.

22. Lacan disagrees with Burke's point about Spinoza's pantheism: "What, quite wrongly, has been thought of in Spinoza as pantheism is simply the reduction of the field of God to the universality of the signifier, which produces a serene, exceptional detachment from human desire. In so far as Spinoza says—*desire is the essence of man*, and in so far as he institutes this desire in the radical dependence of the universality of the signifier, in so far as he does this, he obtains that unique position by which the philosopher—and it is no accident that it is a Jew detached from his tradition who embodies it—may be confused with transcendental love" (*Four Fundamental Concepts* 275).

23. This distinction, along with the charge of being religious "torture porn," would be my critique of Mel Gibson, *The Passion of the Christ*.

24. Such is Kierkegaard's motive, as we will see in the third chapter.

25. I do not mean that the rabbis *abandoned* at some earlier point an Aristotelian notion of the Prime Mover, but rather that, by the late antique at least, a Mover of some sort is not a necessary component of their hermeneutics. The rabbis may in fact have never needed such in the way that Greeks and Christians did. From a Christian perspective, though, the non-necessity would be very strange and, structurally speaking, would seem omitted.

26. Here, I am adapting Giorgio Agamben's understanding of Pauline messianic time by applying it to the rabbinic text instead of the Christian Passion. In my reading, Agamben is insisting on Paul's Judaism against an eschatological Christianity (Agamben).

27. Those who carve time into dispensations, the era between the Passion and the Second Coming—our own, the Church Age—existing in historical time; see Sharon Crowley, *Toward a Civil Discourse: Rhetoric and Fundamentalism* (109).

28. See Gibson, as an easy example. The violent reaction of some Christians to Martin Scorsese, *The Last Temptation of Christ* (may be a read in part as a result of this shift in emphasis.

29. More on trauma is in the fourth chapter.

30. The empty sign is discussed in terms of trauma in the fourth chapter, but a simple notion of it would be a signifier with no signified, or a placeholder for something that can't yet be taken up by/in language.

31. The famous arguments over whether *The Good is Good because God willed it* or *God willed the Good because it is Good* would both work here, since in the former there is a limit to God, a lack even (he can only do Good), and its corrective (the latter) is the splitting of deities so that the Good and God are consubstantial (thus the Logos who exists with God and who God recognizes in Genesis 1 as *good*). Would the Third Person, the Spirit, then be roughly equivalent to God's ego or self-image? Traditionally, the Spirit is God's Love on Earth, and as we saw in the previous chapter, there is something narcissistic about love.

32. And eventually, dispensationalist focus on the eschaton more than the instantiation of Christ, displaying the confusion against which Agamben argues.

33. The metaphor Justin offers is that of fire "which can produce another fire without being diminished" (Boyarin 39); God is thus the Logos's formal, though not temporal, progenitor.

34. See Steven D. Fraade, "Rabbinic Polysemy and Pluralism Revisited: Between Praxis and Thematization."

35. From the *New Oxford Annotated Bible*. Wisdom is often gendered feminine, especially in later discussions of the Shekinah.

36. Boyarin's evidence for Wisdom theology in early Judaism is compelling and certainly too vast to include here. For convincing, look to the entirety of the chapter "The Intertextual Birth of the Logos" in *Borderlines*.

37. See the discussion of Plato in the previous chapter.

38. There isn't space here to broach the question of how the religious practice of the people complicates the relationship, but we might point to the possibility that keeping these commandments, especially those given by the rabbis, is one way to keep the people separate while at the same time allowing a participation in both the past and future glory. One blows the shofar now the way they did back then and will continue to in future generations. Additionally, since there are all sorts of provisions for not following the rules (in the case that following a prescription would injure another person, for instance), these provisions being rules themselves, practice is imminently adaptive toward the particular habitus.

39. Chapter Four will take up Lacanian issues in earnest.

40. The resemblance to classical notions of rhetoric as primarily an oral mode give us even more reason to link rabbinic exegetical practice with a fairly common notion of rhetoric and especially with the sophistic vein. And we still consider virtuosity a hallmark of education; otherwise, why have oral defenses of dissertation, for instance?

41. A friend of mine tells the story of teaching on the fourth floor of a building before elevators were mandatory. A paper was due that day, and ten minutes into class, a student who was very pregnant ran in—out of breath from the stairs—and handed her paper to her instructor. She apologized for interrupting the class, she was in labor and on her way to the hospital, but wanted to make sure the paper was turned in on time!

42. While not applying it to Christianity and Judaism, Kenneth Reinhard reads Lacan's sexuation much the same way in Kenneth Reinhard, "Toward a Political Theology of the Neighbor" (Reinhard and Santner 51-54).

43. I have to admit that in this chapter I may be behaving in much the same way as Žižek does, insofar as an etic approach to rabbinic Judaism as a rhetoric forces, at least for me, sometimes fairly standard rhetorical understandings that find their ancestry in the classically received tradition. For instance, mitzvoth is, for the rabbis, much more than the techne to which I have linked it, and to characterize it solely as such is to read mitzvah in a Greek fashion.

44. In this formulation and from the Christian perspective, the Jew would then be a Christian fantasy, as I explain. For our purposes (and to support my claim that I am not positing an either/or for rhetoric), the two sides should not be read as complementary or in terms of a binary, but rather what I am calling Rabbinic Rhetoric would be supplementary to the Classical.

45. Consider, for instance, Steven F. Kruger, *The Spectral Jew: Conversion and Embodiment in Medieval Europe* (320), or Justin's use of the straw

Jewish man Trypho in the *Dialogue* in order to establish differences between the two "religions" (Martyr).

46. See Timothy Richardson, "Reading, the Masculine: An Orientation of the Community of Readers."

47. I write "humankind" here in order to indicate that, while a masculine noun is used to describe the first human, the sexes have not been set; the word *adam*, generally translated as man, is derived from the word *adamah*, or ground, the dust from which "he" was formed.

48. There is no biblical sense of nature as distinct from God; indeed, there is no word for nature as a clear and separate system, as we find with the Greeks.

49. As a side note, in order to drive home the point of the radical separation of humanity from the divine, the first recorded sacrifice by Cain and Abel is spontaneous. God never asks for it. There is something inherent to the condition of the two brothers, those first born with knowledge of their difference, that makes them want to commune with God. Radical separation is what allows (establishes the conditions for) for worship. Without the separation, God and humans could simply hang out and chat.

50. For an alternate reading of the spatial relation to which she calls attention, as well as a more detailed treatment of sacrifice, see Timothy Richardson, *Divinity in Hindsight: A Structural Evaluation of the Myth of Culture and the Hebrew Origin Narratives* (Lang).

51. If we remember the rough equation made earlier between pain in childbirth and the "natural world" and the linking of this world with the divine, we might discover here part of the rationale that allows Lacan to call one particular face of the other, the "God-face," the feminine.

52. This is really only a clarification, since Kristeva herself stresses the distinction of the two (95).

53. (272). And thus the Word for Girard is the corollary of Longinus's Sublime. The Word (made flesh) is powerful in its absence. See René Girard, Jean-Michel Oughourlian, and Guy Lefort, *Things Hidden Since the Foundation of the World*.

54. Recall Plato's positing love as the recognition of likeness in another. In Lacan's reformulation, love is reflective insofar as I love what is reflected back of me. The subtlety to remember is that a reflection is also always mediated, in this case by what falls away: desire.

55. I have described my position on the nature of lack above, but should point out here that it seems to jibe well with Thomas Rickert's description: "Although nothing is actually lacking in the Real, the effect of symbolization is to introduce lack into all aspects of human affairs." Additionally, Rickert argues, "The upshot is that 'lack' is not a fundamental ontological feature of human beings but the result of the emergence of the subject through language. To put it otherwise, 'lack' refers to the fact that we can never be

entirely autonomous beings." See Thomas J. Rickert, *Acts of Enjoyment: Rhetoric, Žižek, and the Return of the Subject* (Rickert 149). In a way, then, lack is what sutures us to one another and, I'll argue, what makes the fantasy of narrative possible.

56. One cannot then completely fault the student who said that Aristotle knew his Aquinas really well, which obviously made Aristotle Christian. In a special sense, she was right.

57. Such is presumably what certain widespread practices of historicization/interpretation would do; see Girard, for instance.

58. When we do this sort of word association in class on the blackboard, I always begin with "boat" and am still waiting for the class that does not follow with "water." What would a class be like that offered up "gravy"?

59. This is Umberto Eco's example in Umberto Eco's *The Limits of Interpretation* (64).

60. For more on the difference between meaning and knowledge in the context of literature, see Richardson (96).

61. I am not eliminating the possibility of a connection between authorial intention and a produced meaning, but indicating that writing always produced something that is unintended (and unattended): the *something else*.

62. For more on the nature of the event and its representation, though in different terms, see Timothy Richardson, "Brian Eno and the Music of the Spheres: The Possibility of a Postmodern Church" (216-231).

63. This is the logic of the psychoanalytic symptom generally. *Saying*, then, may take on other, symptomatic forms.

64. See Bruce Fink, *The Lacanian Subject: Between Language and Jouissance*, for a discussion of this "second order" trauma (26-28).

65. Another way of describing this lack in the symbolic is, of course, given via castration.

66. For more examples, consider the preparation of knives and especially the binding of the children and the mingling of blood; see Shlomo Eidelberg, *The Jews and the Crusaders: The Hebrew Chronicles of the First and Second Crusades* (31-32).

67. The Lacanian matheme is $\$ \lozenge D$, where the barred or castrated subject recognizes the Other's demand as/for what is apparently available, but which is always contingent.

68. In a way, this logic prefigures Lacan's famous reversal of Dostoyevsky, where Lacan says, "Without God, *nothing* is possible." It is only with the injection of the divine through precedent that the Jews have recourse to any action outside of waiting patiently.

69. $\$ \lozenge a$ is the more common matheme for fantasy, where the barred subject recognizes the object cause of desire as having been lost sometime in the past.

70. So we might take this to mean that, just as a ram was offered as a surrogate for Isaac, so Isaac himself was a surrogate for a ram: a1-a2, the Xs of our previous formulation.

71. Here, perhaps, we touch the Kantian notion of the sublime as it relates to pain.

72. See Colette Soler, "Literature as Symptom" (214). One face of this resistance is certainly the antagonism Žižek points to in narrative. More generically, the enigma is the void, the gap, the caput mortuum, the object *a*.

73. Somewhat cryptically, Lacan states that "the foundation of knowledge is that the jouissance of its exercise is the same as that of its acquisition" (*Encore* 97). In terms of academic enquiry, might this mean that research and writing are the same insofar as they produce the same enjoyment in the face of castration qua joui-sense?

74. The example of the breast and weaning also addresses again the problem with lack first broached in my introduction. Weaning and the lack of the breast only makes sense if there is a prior presence, the breast as object, that is now felt as missing. Of course, all sorts of vulgar psychoanalytic points can be made by tying grown-up lack to weaning, but the primary point here is that there is no lack without a (symbolic or real) presence, since I don't know of many adults who are still breast-fed and one has to assume something like weaning happens even for those of us who were never breast-fed.

75. See Richardson (216-31).

76. Another way of saying this is that the work is always complete vertically (at the level of contingent experience) but never complete horizontally (in terms of narrative).

77. This software combines generative music with a number of (frequently hand-painted) images that overlay each other randomly. The result is the generation of approximately seventy-seven million discrete images.

78. See Chapter 2.1.

79. Via Freud's *Moses and Monotheism*; see Jacques Lacan, *The Ethics of Psychoanalysis* (173-178). Perhaps at this point in Lacan's teaching I have the same complaint I leveled earlier at Žižek. Lacan also sometimes conflates Judaism and Christianity, thus eliding the Jewish.

80. Lacan characterizes the transference relationship (a kind of love) between the analysand and the anaylist as the analysand saying: "I love you, but, because inexplicably I love in you something more than you—the object petit a—I must mutilate you" (*Four Fundamental Concepts* 268).

81. See Lacan's discussion of Richard of Saint Victor and the positing of non-eternal being that is intrinsically so as the signifier placed in contingency (*Encore* 40).

82. A graduate student who is an evangelical minister attended a conference of evangelicals soon after taking my classical rhetoric seminar. He told me later that, as he was listening to some luminary in the field, he began

to realize that the positions the speaker was advocating were really Augustine's positions, but that the speaker and the audience seemed to have no idea that they were old thoughts. This may demonstrate either that there's nothing new under the sun or, more likely, that Christian perspectives in general have very old roots that are so hegemonic that their origins are lost to all but some scholars (and their students).

83. By offering products to me that I didn't know I needed before the commercial, advertizing does much the same job, and certainly advertizing has something to do with rhetoric.

84. See Chapter Two on the master/servant relationship via Žižek.

85. Levi Bryant and I have been discussing the assumed animosity between Deleuze & Guattari and Lacan (at least, as it has been assumed in rhetoric studies since the 1980s) and suspect that the assumption arises from an accident of translation. The works of Deleuze & Guattari were translated fairly quickly, when only a few early works and seminars of Lacan's were available in English. That is, none of his work on the Real that inspired so much of French intellectual thought and production from the late 1960s could be read by many in the US. As much as Deleuze and Guattari are still useful, work needs to be done in rereading them in light of the recent translations *Encore* (1998) and *The Other Side of Psychoanalysis* (2006). My reading is that they are not so very far apart.

86. Writing, Bracher argues, often promotes such consolidation. I would suggest that such is not the goal of psychoanalysis, but perhaps of American-style ego psychology.

87. This kind of activism may be what Michael Bérubé sees as the university's project when he writes:

> Personally, I wish we worked even better, and that our graduates emerged from our institutions even more cosmopolitan, less parochial, more willing to consider themselves citizens of (and responsible to) the entire world, more prepared for the moral and intellectual consequences of globalization; I wish our graduates were more fluent writers and more nimble thinkers; I wish more of them majored in the liberal arts, and that more of my fellow citizens appreciated the strength of liberalism, the power of the arts, and the appeal of liberal arts. But when I'm discouraged about such things, I take some solace in the fact, that despite it all, and despite the best efforts of the anti-academic right, universities remain among the most respected institutions in American life, ranking far above organized religion, big business, Congress, the legal profession, and the news media—and just above the White House and the Supreme Court.

88. See Michael Bérubé, *What's Liberal About the Liberal Arts?: Classroom Politics and "Bias" in Higher Education* (281).

Works Cited

Agamben, Giorgio. "The Time That Is Left." *Epoche* 7.1 (2002): 1-14. Web. 16 Feb. 2012.
Anderson, Bernhard W., Bruce Manning Metzger, and Roland Edmund Murphy. *The New Oxford Annotated Bible with the Apocryphal/Deuterocanonical Books.* New York: Oxford UP, 1991. Print.
Aristotle, and Harold Percy Cooke. *The Organon: On Interpretation.* Trans. Harold Percy Cooke. Cambridge, MA: Harvard UP, 1962. Print.
Aristotle, and George Alexander Kennedy. *On Rhetoric: A Theory of Civic Discourse.* New York: Oxford UP, 1991. Print.
Aristotle. *The Complete Works of Aristotle: The Revised Oxford Translation.* Trans. Jonathan Barnes. Princeton, N.J: Princeton UP, 1985. Print.
Augustine, and R. P. H. Green. *On Christian Teaching.* Oxford [u.a.]: Oxford UP, 1999. Print.
Augustine, and Garry Wills. *Confessions.* New York: Penguin Books, 2006. Print.
Baudrillard, Jean. *The Illusion of the End.* Stanford, Calif.: Stanford UP, 1994. Print.
Bérubé, Michael. *What's Liberal about the Liberal Arts?: Classroom Politics and "Bias" in Higher Education.* 1st ed. New York: W.W. Norton, 2006. Print..
Bloom, Harold. *The Anxiety of Influence: A Theory of Poetry.* 2nd ed. New York: Oxford UP, 1997. Print.
Boyarin, Daniel. *Border Lines: The Partition of Judaeo-Christianity.* Philadelphia, PA: U of Pennsylvania P, 2004. Print.
Boyd, Brian. *Nabokov's Ada: The Place of Consciousness.* Ann Arbor, MI: Ardis, 1985. Print.
Bracher, Mark. *The Writing Cure: Psychoanalysis, Composition, and the Aims of Education.* Carbondale: Southern Illinois UP, 1999. Print.
Bryant, Levi R. *Difference and Givenness: Deleuze's Transcendental Empiricism and the Ontology of Immanence.* Evanston, Ill.: Northwestern UP, 2008. Print.
Burke, Kenneth. *A Grammar of Motives.* Berkeley, CA: U of California P, 1969a. Print.
—. *A Rhetoric of Motives.* Berkeley, CA: U of California P, 1969b. Print.
—. *The Rhetoric of Religion.* Berkeley, CA: U of California P, 1961c. Print.

—. *The Rhetoric of Religion: Studies in Logology.* Berkeley: U of California P, 1970d. Print.
Caruth, Cathy. *Unclaimed Experience: Trauma, Narrative, and History.* Baltimore, MD: Johns Hopkins UP, 1996. Print.
Chaitin, Gilbert D. *Rhetoric and Culture in Lacan.* Vol. 19. New York: Cambridge UP, 1996. Print.
Crowley, Sharon. *Toward a Civil Discourse: Rhetoric and Fundamentalism.* Pittsburgh, PA: U of Pittsburgh P, 2006. Print.
Deleuze, Gilles. *Difference and Repetition* New York: Columbia UP, 1994. Print.
Deleuze, Gilles, and Félix Guattari. *Anti-Oedipus: Capitalism and Schizophrenia.* Minneapolis, MI: U of Minnesota P, 1983. Print.
Dolgopolski, Sergey B. *What is Talmud?: The Art of Disagreement.* New York: Fordham UP, 2009. Print.
Eco, Umberto. *The Limits of Interpretation.* Bloomington, IN: Indiana UP, 1990. Print.
Eden, Kathy. *Hermeneutics and the Rhetorical Tradition: Chapters in the Ancient Legacy and its Humanist Reception.* New Haven: Yale UP, 1997. Print.
Eidelberg, Shlomo. *The Jews and the Crusaders: The Hebrew Chronicles of the First and Second Crusades.* Madison, MI: U of Wisconsin P, 1977. Print.
Eliot, Thomas Stearns. "Tradition and the Individual Talent." *The Sacred Wood: Essays on Poetry and Criticism.* London: Methuen, 1950. Print.
Eno, Brian, and Jonathan Carter. "Centuries of Art at the Baltic [Interview]." *BBC Collective.* February 8 2007. Web. 16 Feb. 2012.
Eno, Brian. *77 Million Paintings.* All Saints, 2006a. DVD-Video.
—. *A Year with Swollen Appendices: Brian Eno's Diary.* London: Faber and Faber, 1996b. Print.
Fink, Bruce. *The Lacanian Subject: Between Language and Jouissance.* Princeton, NJ: Princeton UP, 1995. Print.
Fraade, Steven D. "Rabbinic Polysemy and Pluralism Revisited: Between Praxis and Thematization." *AJS Review* 31.1 (2007): 1-40. Web. 16 Feb. 2012.
Fulcher of Chartes. "Urban II: Speech at Council of Clermont, 1095." *A Source Book for Medieval History.* Oliver J. Thatcher and Edgar Holmes McNeal, Eds. New York: Scribners, 1905. Print.
The Passion of the Christ. Dir. Gibson, Mel. Perf. Davey, Bruce, Stephen McEveety, Benedict Fitzgerald, et al. 20th Century Fox Home Entertainment, 2004. Film.
Girard, René, Jean-Michel Oughourlian, and Guy Lefort. *Things Hidden since the Foundation of the World.* Stanford, Calif.: Stanford UP, 1987. Print.
Reptile Boy. Dir. Greenwalt, David. Perf. Gellar, Sarah Michelle, Nicholas Brendon, Alyson Hannigan, et al. 20th Century Fox, 2006. Film.

Handelman, Susan A. *The Slayers of Moses: The Emergence of Rabbinic Interpretation in Modern Literary Theory*. Albany, NY: SUNY P, 1982. Print.

Harman, Graham. *Prince of Networks : Bruno Latour and Metaphysics*. Prahran, Vic: Re-press, 2009. Print.

Hidary, Richard. "Classical Rhetorical Tradition and Reasoning in the Talmud: The Case of Yerushalmi Berakhot 1:1." *AJS Review* 34.1 (2010): 33. Print.

Hughes, Aaron W., and Elliot R. Wolfson. *New Directions in Jewish Philosophy*. Bloomington: Indiana UP, 2010. Print.

Jaffee, Martin S. "Spoken, Written, Incarnate: Ontologies of Textuality in Classical Rabbinic Judaism." *Voice, Text, Hypertext: Emerging Practices in Textual Studies*. Ed. Raimonda Modiano, Leroy F. Searle, and Peter Shillingsburg. New York, NY: Palgrave Macmillan, 2004. 83-100. Print.

Justin Martyr and Thomas B. Falls. *Dialogue with Typho*. Washington D. C.: Catholic U of America P, 2003. Print.

Kennedy, George Alexander. *Classical Rhetoric and its Christian and Secular Tradition from Ancient to Modern Times*. 2, rev and enl ed. Chapel Hill, NC: U of North Carolina P, 1999. Print.

Krey, August C., ed. *The First Crusade: The Accounts of Eyewitnesses and Participants*. Princeton, NJ: Princeton UP, 1921. Print.

Kristeller, Paul Oskar, and Michael Mooney. *Renaissance Thought and its Sources*. New York: Columbia UP, 1979. Print.

Kristeva, Julia. *Powers of Horror: An Essay on Abjection*. New York: Columbia UP, 1982. Print.

Kruger, Steven F. *The Spectral Jew: Conversion and Embodiment in Medieval Europe*. Vol. 40. Minneapolis, MN: U of Minnesota P, 2006. Print.

Your Friends and Neighbors. Dir. LaBute, Neil. Polygram, 1998. Film.

Lacan, Jacques. *Encore: The Seminar of Jacques Lacan*. Trans. Bruce Fink. Ed. Jacques-Alain Miller. Vol. Book XX. New York: Norton, 1998a. Print.

—. *The Ethics of Psychoanalysis, 1959-1960*. 1 American ed. Vol. Book VII. New York: Norton, 1992b. Print.

—. *The Four Fundamental Concepts of Psycho-Analysis*. Trans. Alan Sheridan. Ed. Jacques-Alain Miller. New York: Norton, 1981c. Print.

—. *The Other Side of Psychoanalysis*. Vol. Book XVII. New York: Norton, 2006d. Print..

Shoah. Dir. Lanzmann, Claude. Pref. Anonymous New Yorker Video, 1985. Film.

Liebersohn, Yousef Z. "Rhetoric: Art and Pseudo-Art in Plato's *Gorgias*." *Arethusa* 38 (2005): 303-29. Print.

Linck, Matthew S. "Unmastering Speech: Irony in Plato's 'Phaedrus'." *Philosophy and Rhetoric* 36.3 (2003): 264-76. Print.

Lyotard, Jean-François. "Answering the Question: What is Postmodernism?" *The Postmodern Condition: A Report on Knowledge.* Minneapolis, MN: U of Minnesota P, 1993. Print.

Marcus, Ivan. "From Politics to Martyrdom: Shifting Paradigms in the Hebrew Narratives of the 1096 Crusade Riots." *Prooftexts* 2 (1982): 40-52. Print.

Menotti, Massimo and Francesca. E-Mails to the Author. 27 Apr. and 3 May 1998. Email.

Metzger, David. *The Lost Cause of Rhetoric: The Relation of Rhetoric and Geometry in Aristotle and Lacan.* Carbondale, IL: Southern Illinois UP, 1995. Print.

Midrash Rabbah: Genesis. Trans. H. Freedman. London: Soncino P, 1983. Print.

Nabokov, Vladimir Vladimirovich. *Bend Sinister.* New York: Time-Life Books, 1964. Print.

—. *The Gift.* New York: Putnam, 1963. Print.

—. *Lectures on Literature.* New York: Harcourt Brace Jovanovich, 1980a. Print.

—. *A Russian Beauty and Other Stories.* 1st ed. New York: McGraw-Hill, 1973b. Print.

—. *Strong Opinions.* New York: McGraw-Hill, 1973c. Print.

Orgazmo. Dir. Parker, Trey. Prod. Kuzui Fran Rubel. Kuzui Enterprises, 1997. Film.

Pesikta Rabbati: Discourses for Feasts, Fasts, and Special Sabbaths. Trans. William G. Braude. Vol. 18. New Haven, CT: Yale UP, 1968. Print.

Plato. *Plato on Rhetoric and Language: Four Key Dialogues.* Ed. Jean Nienkamp. Mahwah, NJ: Hermagoras P, 1999. Print.

Pynchon, Thomas. *The Crying of Lot 49.* New York: Harper and Row, 1990. Print.

Rashi, et al. [Perush Rashi 'al Ha-Torah] = *Rashi: The Torah with Rashi's Commentary.* 1st ed. Brooklyn, N.Y.: Mesorah Publications, 1999. Print.

Reineke, Martha Jane. *Sacrificed Lives: Kristeva on Women and Violence.* Bloomington, IN: Indiana UP, 1997. Print.

Reinhard, Kenneth. "Toward a Political Theology of the Neighbor." *The Neighbor: Three Inquiries in Political Theology.* Ed. Slavoj Žižek, Eric Santner, and Kenneth Reinhard. Chicago, IL: U of Chicago P, 2005. Print.

Richardson, Timothy. "Brian Eno and the Music of the Spheres: The Possibility of a Postmodern Church." *Medievalism and the Academy II: Medievalism and Cultural Studies.* Ed. David Metzger. London: Boydell and Brewer, 1999. 216-231. Print.

—. "Divinity in Hindsight: A Structural Evaluation of the Myth of Culture and the Hebrew Origin Narratives." *Semiotics 1994: The Proceedings of*

the *19th Annual Meeting of the Semiotic Society of America.* 20-23 October 1994. Print.
—. "Reading, the Masculine: An Orientation of the Community of Readers." *Literature and Psychology* 44.1 (1998): 96. Print.
Rickert, Thomas J. *Acts of Enjoyment: Rhetoric, Žižek, and the Return of the Subject.* Pittsburgh, Pa.: U of Pittsburgh P, 2007. Print.
The Last Temptation of Christ. Dir. Scorsese, Martin. Pref. Anonymous Cineplex-Odeon Films, 1988. Film.
Sifre: A Tannaitic Commentary on the Book of Deuteronomy. Trans. Reuven Hammer. Vol. 24. New Haven: Yale UP, 1986. Print.
Soler, Colette. "Literature as Symptom." *Lacan and the Subject of Language. Ed.* Ed. Ellie Ragland-Sullivan and Mark Bracher. New York: Routledge, 1991. Print.
Soncino Talmud Davka Corp, 2001. CD-ROM.
Stern, David. *Midrash and Theory: Ancient Jewish Exegesis and Contemporary Literary Studies.* Evanston, IL: Northwestern UP, 1996. Print.
Taylor, Charles. *A Secular Age.* Cambridge, MA: Belknap Press of Harvard UP, 2007. Print.
Vitanza, Victor J. *Negation, Subjectivity, and the History of Rhetoric.* Albany: SUNY P, 1997. Print.
Widder, Nathan. "What's Lacking in the Lack: A Comment on the Virtual." *Angelaki: Journal of the Theoretical Humanities* 5.3 (2000): 117. Print.
Žižek, Slavoj. *On Belief.* New York: Routledge, 2001a. Print.
—. *The Plague of Fantasies.* London: Verso, 1997b. Print.
—. *The Puppet and the Dwarf: The Perverse Core of Christianity.* Cambridge, MA: MIT P, 2003c. Print.
—. *The Sublime Object of Ideology.* London: Verso, 1989d. Print.
Zohar. Trans. Harry Sperling and Maurice Simon. Vol. II. London: Soncino P, 1949. Print.

Index

Agamben, Giorgio, 156
Albert of Aix, 112
Aristotle, ix–x, 9, 18, 27– 31, 33–35, 46, 51–52, 62, 109, 141, 153n4, 155n17, 159n56
Augustine, 3, 9, 18, 29, 33– 36, 39, 40–41, 43, 45–46, 48, 50–51, 61–62, 65, 71, 85, 88, 99–100, 141, 154n11, 161n82

Baudrillard, Jean, 53, 107, 108, 134
Bérubé, Michael, 161
Boyarin, Daniel, 8, 10, 43, 49, 55–59, 62, 65, 71, 157n36; *Border Lines*; *The Partition of Judaeo–Christianity*, 8, 71
Bracher, Mark, 147, 161n86
Bryant, Levi, 153n7, 161n85
Buffy the Vampire Slayer, 132, 141
Burke, Kenneth, x, 5, 9–11, 18, 20, 28–29, 31–34, 36, 37–43, 51, 96–99, 102, 107, 134–135, 148, 155n22; *Grammar of Motives*, 31–33, 51; *A Rhetoric of Motives*, 5, 18, 20, 29, 33, 96; *The Rhetoric of Religion*, x, 7, 21, 37, 39, 42–43, 154n11, 155n18-19

caput mortuum, 126, 131–133, 160
cause, 41, 109–110, 119; and effect, 113–114, 121; efficient, 36, 46, 51, 54, 102, 137, 152, 155n19; extimate, 7, 12, 14, 18, 150; extrinsic, 7–9, 11–12, 18, 44, 65, 69, 141, 150; final, 4, 46, 51, 54, 102, 137, 139, 152, 155n19; formal/logical/necessary, 27, 31–32, 54, 94, 109, 125, 133, 137, 140, 152; missing, 60, 78, 99, 100–105, 125, 134, 136–139, 151; object (*a*, of desire), 94–95, 97, 100, 110, 129–130, 135, 140, 146–148, 151
Caruth, Cathy, 13, 106–110, 134, 138–139
Chaitin, Gilbert, 108, 130, 138
Christianity, ix, 8–10, 12, 18, 33, 36, 40, 56–58, 66, 71, 79, 117, 143, 156n26, 157n42, 160n79; Christian, x, 8–9, 18, 21, 33–34, 36–37, 41–44, 46, 53–54, 56, 58, 60, 67, 69, 71, 72, 85–86, 91–92, 99, 101–102, 112–113, 118, 139, 144, 148, 154, 157, 159n56, 161n82; Passion of Christ, 36, 41, 42, 46, 50–51, 55, 62, 72, 78, 85–86, 91, 99, 118, 125, 155n17and 19, 156n23, 156n 26, 156n 27
Chronicle of Solomon bar Simson, x, 13, 111–112, 114, 115–117, 119, 122–124
contingency, 5, 7, 9, 30, 42, 52, 55, 62, 102, 127, 141–143, 152, 160n81

169

Crowley, Sharon, 54–55, 127, 142, 144, 147–149, 156n27

Deleuze, Gilles, 12, 145–146, 153n7, 161n85

Eno, Brian, 136–137, 141, 148, 151, 159n62; *77 Million Paintings*, 137; *Music for Prague*, 136–137

Fink, Bruce, 118, 131, 132, 141, 144, 146, 159n64
Fraade, Steven, 56–57, 156

Girard, René, x, 11, 75–79, 84–96, 99–102, 124, 158n53, 159n57

Handelman, Susan, 20, 30, 32, 46, 60, 126, 143–144
Harmon, Graham, 155n20
Hidary, Richard, 8

immanence, ix, 10–11, 65, 70,

Jaffee, Martin, 67, 69
Judaism, ix, 7–10, 40, 56–57, 66–67, 69, 71–72, 79, 83, 117, 156n26, 157n36, 157n 42, 157n 43, 160n79

Kennedy, George Alexander, 19, 26, 153–155
Kierkegaard, Søren, x, 11, 95–101, 134–135, 156n24
Kristeller, P. O., 17
Kristeva, Julia, x, 11, 78–84, 89–96, 99–101, 108, 124, 132, 135, 158n52; abject, 7, 79, 82, 84, 89–92, 100, 108, 130, 132
Kruger, Steven F., 157n45

LaBute, Neil: *Your Friends and Neighbors*, 24
Lacan, Jacques, 7–12, 14–15; academic discourse, 125, 130; discourse, 128, 129; *Encore; The Seminar of Jacques Lacan*, 70, 73, 95, 98, 114, 120, 128, 133, 140–141, 144–146, 149, 160n73 and 81, 161n85; *Ethics of Psychoanalysis*, 13, 139, 160n79; *Four Fundamental Concepts of Psycho–Analysis*, 119, 140, 154n13, 155n22, 160n80; jouissance, ix, 10–13, 98, 100–111, 118, 122–125, 135, 139, 140, 146, 160; object *a*, 91, 108, 111, 125, 139–140, 146, 151, 160; Other, ix–x, 6–7, 11, 55, 66, 69, 70–73, 89–90, 98–100, 107, 118–119, 123–124, 130, 134, 137–141, 144–147, 151, 158n51, 159n67; *Other Side of Psychoanalysis*, 145–146, 161n85; sexuation, 69–72, 134, 140, 157n42
lack, 11–13, 22–23, 25, 27, 37, 41, 55, 70, 72, 90, 94–95, 98–100, 101, 106, 109–110, 111, 120–122, 124, 130, 134, 136–138, 141, 144–145, 148, 0153n7, 154n13, 156n31, 158n55, 159n65, 160n74,
Linck, Mathew S., 154n12
logos, 26, 69, 72, 139, 143; and love, 2, 40, 51, 54, 65, 95, 154n11, 156n31; Johannine, 58, 87–89; Logos Asarkos, 58–59; Logos Ensarkos, 42, 58–59, 62, 72, 139, 143; two powers, 57–59 ; Word, 18, 34–40, 42, 50, 55–59, 84–93, 99, 102, 126, 143
Longinus, 18, 23–26, 74, 86, 95, 99–100, 137, 141, 158n53

love, x, xiii, 6–11, 14, 75, 78, 93–99,125; Platonic, 21–27, 94, 99, 129; Christian, 37–43, 46, 51, 54, 65, 72, 84–89, 99, 102, 139–140, 154n11, 156n31; rabbinic, 72–73, 102, 120, 124, ; psychoanalysis and, 129–30, 144, 146–147, 152, 155n22. 158n54, 160n80
Lyotard, Jean-François, 108, 135–138

Marcus, Ivan, 111–119, 123
Metzger, David, ix, 9, 29
Midrash Rabbah, ix, 50–52, 59, 63, 68

Nabokov, Vladimir, 3–5, 10, 14–15, 128; *The Gift*, 3, 153n1
narrative, 31, 76, 96, 99–100, 111–125; Christian, 36, 41; and psychoanalysis, 106–107, 110, 120, 131–132, 135–136; rabbinic 54, 57, 59–60, 63
necessity, 7, 9, 36, 51, 59, 93, 102, 119, 133, 152

Pesikta Rabbati, 49
Plato, ix, 3, 9, 14, 17–27, 30, 31, 42, 46, 64, 95, 99–100, 129, 141, 149–150, 153n9, 157n37, 158n54; *Gorgias*, 19–20, 154n10; *Phaedrus*, 20–25, 31, 64, 94, 129, 154n12
Pope Urban II, 113
Pynchon, Thomas, 126

Rabbinic Judaism, ix–xi, 8–10, 14–15, 44–73, 103, 133, 141–143, 150, 153n5, 156n26, 156n34, 157n40, 157n43, 157n44
Rashi, 116, 120, 123
Reineke, Martha, 84
Reinhard, Kenneth, xiii, 157
Richardson, Timothy, ix–x, 136–138, 158n46, 158n50, 159n60, 159n 62, 160n75
Rickert, Thomas, 158n55

sacrifice, x, 11, 41–42, 75–86, 90, 93–95, 98–111, 115, 118–124, 132, 158n50; Binding of Isaac, 11, 96, 116, 119–124
Sifre: A Tannaitic Commentary on the Book of Deuteronomy, 45, 65
Sifre Deuteronomy, 45, 65
Soler, Colette, 126, 160n72
Stern, David, 45, 50

Talmud, Babylonian, ix, 10, 45–49, 57, 61, 65, 73
Taylor, Charles, 148, 155n21
Torah, ix, 45–50, 56, 59–70, 73, 139; Oral, 43, 48–49, 56, 60–62, 71; Written, 51, 60, 139

Vitanza, Victor, xiii, 136

Widder, Nathan, 153n6

Žižek, Slavoj, 40, 43, 53, 55, 59–61, 66, 71–72, 110, 118–123, 127, 130, 140, 151, 157n43, 159n55, 160n72, 160n79, 161n84
Zohar, 63–64

About the Author

Timothy Richardson's work has appeared in such journals as *JAC*, *Kairos*, *Pre/Text*, *Paris Review*, and *Western Humanities Review*. He is Associate Professor of English at the University of Texas at Arlington, where he teaches courses in antique and contemporary rhetorics, psychoanalytic theory, media studies, and writing. He lives in Fort Worth, Texas with his wife, fiction writer Laura Kopchick, and their two children Harper and Ben.

www.ingramcontent.com/pod-product-compliance
Lightning Source LLC
Chambersburg PA
CBHW021858230426
43671CB00006B/440